China's Financial System

Dominique De Rambures • Felipe Escobar Duenas

China's Financial System

Growth and Inefficiency

palgrave
macmillan

Dominique De Rambures
Master Banque Finance
Paris I University Panthéon Sorbonne
Paris, France

Felipe Escobar Duenas
Master Banque Finance
Paris I University Panthéon Sorbonne
Paris, France

ISBN 978-3-319-40450-9 ISBN 978-3-319-40451-6 (eBook)
DOI 10.1007/978-3-319-40451-6

Library of Congress Control Number: 2017930599

Cover illustration: Mode Images / Alamy Stock Photo
Cover Design: Liron Gilenberg

Printed on acid-free paper

This Palgrave Macmillan imprint is published by Springer Nature
The registered company is Springer International Publishing AG
The registered company address is: Gewerbestrasse 11, 6330 Cham, Switzerland

Contents

List of Abbreviations and Acronyms

ABC	Agricultural Bank of China
ADA	Abu Dhabi Investment Agency
ADB	Asia Development Bank
AIIB	Asia Infrastructure Investment Bank
AMC	Asset Management Company
ANZ	Australian & New Zealand Bank
APEC	Asia Pacific Economic Cooperation
AVIC	Aviation Industry Corp.
B2B	Business-to-Business
BBVA	Banco de Bilbao Viscaya Argentaria
BEIC	British East India Company
BMG	Beijing Municipal Government
BOC	Bank of China
BOCOM	Bank of Communications
BRICS	Brazil, Russia, India, China, South Africa
C2C	Consumer-to-Consumer
CBRC	China Banking Regulatory Commission
CCB	China Construction Bank
CCP	Chinese Communist Party
CCT	China Credit Trust
CD	Certificate of Deposit
CDB	China Development Bank

CEXIM	China Export and Import Bank
CIBIC	Commercial and Industrial Bank of China
CIC	China Investment Corp.
CICC	China International Capital Corp.
CIDM	China Insurance Deposit Mechanism
CIRC	China Insurance Regulatory Commission
CITIC	China International Trust and Investment Corp.
CNAPS	China National Advanced Payment System
CNCC	China National Nuclear Corp.
CNIG	China National Investment & Guarantee Co Ltd
CNPC	China National Petroleum Corp.
COSCO	China Ocean Shipping Cy.
CP Group	Chaoren Pokphand Group
CPB	Consumer Protection Bureau
CPIC	China Power Industrial Corp.
CSI	China Shipbuilding Corp.
CSPG	China Southern Power Grid
CSRC	China Securities Regulatory Commission
CSSC	China State Shipbuilding Corp.
DVP	Delivery versus Payment
ECB	European Central Bank
EFT	Exchange Traded Fund
EM	Europay
EMS	European Monetary System
FCPB	Financial Consumer Protection Bureau
FDI	Foreign Direct Investment
FSA	Financial Supervision Agency
FSR	IMF Financial Stability Report
FTAAP	Free Trade Area of Asia Pacific
GITIC	Guangdong Investment and Trust Company
Guotai	Guotai Junan Securities Co.
HKE	Hong Kong Securities Exchange and Clearing Ltd
HKMA	Hong Kong Monetary Authority
HKSE	Hong Kong Stock Exchange
HKSFE	Hong Kong Securities and Futures Commission
HPVS	High Value Payment System

HSBC	Hong Kong and Shanghai Bank Co.
HUIJIN	Central Huijin Investment Co.
IBRD	International Bank for Reconstruction and Development
IBOC	International Bank of China
ICBC	Industrial and Commercial Bank of China
IFC	International Finance Company
IIBA	Infrastructure Investment Asian Bank
IMF	International Monetary Fund
IPO	Initial Public Offering
Jiany	China Jiany Investment Ltd.
KKR	Kohlberg Kravis Robert
LGFVs	Local Government Financing Vehicles
LME	London Metal Exchange
MDE	Mainland Designated Companies
MOF	Ministry of Finance
MOR	Ministry of Railways
MSCI	Morgan Stanley Commodity Index
NASDAQ	National Association of Securities Dealers Automated Quotation
NCSSF	National Council of Social Security Fund
NDB	New Development Bank
NDRC	National Development and Reform Commission
NSSF	National Social Security Fund
NYSE	New York Stock Exchange
P2P	Peer-to-Peer (or Person-to-Person)
PBOC	People's Bank of China
PICC	People's Insurance Company of China
PMC	Party Military Commission
PSBC	Postal Savings Bank of China
PwC	Price WaterhouseCoopers
QFII	Qualified Foreign Institutional Investors
QIA	Quatar Investment Agency
RBS	Royal Bank of Scotland
RDSC	Research Department of the State Council
ROE	Return on Equity
RQFII	Renminbi Qualified Foreign Institutional Investors

RTGS	Real Time Gross Settlement System
SAFE	State Agency of Foreign Exchange
SAMA	Saudi Arabia Monetary Agency
SASAC	State Owned Asset Supervision and Administration Commission
SCO	Shanghai Cooperation Organization
SDR	Special Drawing Rights
SEA	Special Economic Area
SEC	Security and Exchange Commission
SEZ	Special Economic Zone
SIC	Government of Singapore Investment Corp.
SMEs	Small and Medium-sized Enterprises
SOE	State Owned Enterprise
SSE	Shanghai Stock Exchange
SWF	Sovereign Wealth Fund
SWIFT	Society for Worldwide Interbank Financial Telecommunication
TIC	Trust and Investment Company
TPG	TPG Capital fund (ex Texas Pacific Group)
TPP	Trans Pacific Partnership
TVE	Township & Village Enterprise
WMP	Wealth Management Products
WTO	World Trade Organization

List of Figures

List of Tables

1

Introduction

Before addressing the strengths and weaknesses of its financial system, it is worth remembering that China experienced one of the fastest growth rates over a long period (an average of 10% a year over 30 years, 1978–2008). It was much higher than England during the Industrial Revolution (less than 1% a year over a century) [1]. Based on its economic and social achievements, the Chinese economy is by far the most effective. In 2015, China was outperformed only by India (7.5% as opposed to 6.9%), although India started far behind and from a much lower level. However, the Chinese growth model that triggered such a remarkable economic performance, thanks to a combination of market and State stimuli, might well be the cause of the steadily declining growth rate and the deteriorating growth model.

The policy of reform and opening up initiated in 1972 by Deng Xiao ping has progressively extended: from the agricultural field (household contracts) to the industrial one, from the people's communes and State owned industries to private companies, and more recently to the banking and financial sector. The Chinese financial Big Bang took place in the first decade of the 2000s as a follow up to the wave of privatization of State owned banks and companies. The control of the financial

D. De Rambures, F. Escobar Duenas, *China's Financial System*,
DOI 10.1007/978-3-319-40451-6_1

industry is naturally a power struggle between political factions. Today, the allocation of key positions mirrors the political strength of the challenging teams (princelings, Shanghai gang, Party Youth Movement, Party school and research centres, regional connections, etc.). Furthermore, the issue of banking and finance is a critical one between pro-market "reformists" and pro-State "conservatives", although such a Western distinction is somewhat biased, as most Chinese leaders are both "reformists" in economic terms and "conservatives" in political terms.

However, an increasing set of worrying clues casts doubt over a sustainable growth model: growing inequalities, pollution, spreading corruption, increasing number of migrants who have no access to social benefits, unemployed graduate youth, fast-growing indebtedness, overcapacities and swelling inventories, loss-making State owned companies that are kept alive, increasing rate of bank non-performing loans, and so on. The growth rate is declining steadily from its peak of 10% in 2010 down to 6.9% in 2015. The investment growth rate is rising twice as fast as the GDP growth rate. As a result, global indebtedness skyrocketed from 127% of GDP in 2008 to 247% in 2015. So far, the growing levels of debt have been absorbed, thanks to the high level of savings (53% of the GDP), much higher than the investment rate (37% of the GDP) that led to accumulated foreign exchange reserves far above what is needed. It is now obvious that the record growth rate over such a long period of time was primarily due to a catch-up effect. Apart from the institutional causes that will be seen later on, the natural law of decreasing returns should, sooner or later, lead to a decreasing growth rate.

In view of avoiding the "middle-income trap", China must change from one growth model to another: from an investment and export-led economy to an internal demand-driven economy, i.e. increasing household consumption and living standards, from manufacturing industries to service industries, from public to private investments funded by public savings rather than by State owned banks, from a world's work power and assembly line producing mass consumption products, to a new range of products incorporating more value added and thus enabling a climb up the value chain.

The 12th (2011–2015) and the 13th (2016–2020) Five-Year Plans have addressed the issue by listing the ways and means to move from being a developing country to becoming a developed "middle income" country. Chinese leaders keep stating that the Chinese economy should be increasingly driven and regulated by market forces. However, a set of crises over the last few years have led to a questioning of the Plans' targets and the development of market mechanisms: in June 2013 a monetary crisis drove the market rate up to 10% and wrecked the interbank market. In June 2015, the foreign exchange crisis burned $1 trillion foreign exchange reserves within a few months and triggered the devaluation of the yuan; and in August 2015 a stock crisis entailed a 30% fall in stock prices and the withdrawal of foreign investors. The crisis factors, still being operating factors, mean that the market crisis remains unresolved leading to far-reaching consequences.

The decreasing growth rate and investment rate of return, the repeated market crises and the high market volatility, cast doubt over the efficiency of the financial system, i.e. the optimum allocation of resources, the capacity to collect public savings to be allocated to the most profitable investments at the lowest cost to the benefit of the whole country. According to the Austrian economist, Friedrich Hayek (1899–1992), the market price has two functions: an information function and a regulation function. The former may be more important than the latter. By producing biased information and twisted prices, Chinese markets do not fulfil their basic functions.

However, financial markets like the credit market are tightly linked to each other. Banks turn deposits into loans. Stock exchanges convert savings into investments. Stock and credit markets are tightly dependent on the cash market. Stock and bond markets are tightly dependent on bank credit. And so on. If markets are not properly connected, if moving from one asset to another is not quick, easy and costless, the price transmission mechanism does not work. In the event of a market imbalance, there are no market forces to draw back and flatten price fluctuations. In China, bank lending is reserved for State companies and large private groups closely connected to the Party and the government. The private companies and small companies that provide 80% of jobs and investments have to turn to the credit black market (the "informal" market). As long as the implicit State guarantee is taken for granted, as long as the government is backing loss-making State owned ("zombie") companies, as long as the government is bailing out bankrupted banks, trusts and companies, investors will not make a difference to the overall range of risk and creditworthiness. The investment decision is not grounded on profit record and prospects, but on State connections. There is no moral hazard in Chinese markets.

At this stage of development, the issue is no longer an economic one but a political one. The move from one growth model to another is a political matter which involves Party and government institutions. In China, politics and economics are one and the same thing. The State Council, the highest government body, acts as a referee between conflicting agents. As a result, the final decision is taken on political grounds. Between social and political stability on one side, and the settlement of a market crisis on the other, the Party-State has always leant towards the former. Reforms are postponed until the situation is more stable.

Accordingly, we will start by studying the Chinese decision making process in economic, financial and monetary areas (Chaps. 2 and 3), before we go through the banking sector (Chaps. 4, 5, 6, and 7) and financial markets (Chaps. 8 and 9) to end up with the foreign exchange markets (Chap. 10).

Reference

1. Maddison, Angus. 2001. *The World Economy: A Millennial Perspective*. Paris: OECD.

2

China's Decision Making System

It may sound strange to begin a book about the Chinese financial system with a description of the decision making system, but in China, everything is "political". Politics and economics are one and the same thing. There is no Chinese wall between the State and the market, as is customary in a market economy. The decision making system is not transparent, which makes it difficult for the markets to work properly. According to the Constitution, China is a centralized one-party system. The Chinese Communist Party (CCP) controls directly or indirectly everyone and everything. But if the Party is powerful, it is not limitless: it generates counter-balances from within the Party and the State apparatus. Central government action is limited by the sheer size of the country and the population: 1.3 billion people scattered over 6 million square miles. The Party-State has to cope with a multi-layered bureaucracy: provinces, county, districts, towns, villages. Some towns are so large that they form a single autonomous unit (Beijing, Shanghaî, Chongking). The Party secretary of a province is much more influential than a minister based in Beijing. In theory, the flow of instructions goes down while the flow of information goes up, but the Centre must come to terms with the passive resistance of local levels and inaccuracy of the information. The deadly

D. De Rambures, F. Escobar Duenas, *China's Financial System*,
DOI 10.1007/978-3-319-40451-6_2

famine of the Great Leap Forward in the 1960s was caused not only by Mao's megalomania, but also by the flow of reports channelled from local officials to the top, each one outbidding the lower one throughout the upper level. Although 95% of the Chinese population belongs to the Han ethnic group, the Chinese do not understand each other and have to rely upon a common language, Mandarin. Local idiosyncrasies are very strong. Local dialects, regional patrons, family links are alternative sources of power. A Party official appointed in a remote area has to cope with local powers and local leaders whom he does not understand. In any case he expects to be moved to a new appointment within two or three years. The central government is also limited by the bureaucracy at both the central and local level. Any company manager must come to terms with the overwhelming network of 80 million civil servants and as many party members (even though some are both). Any private entrepreneur has to rely upon a wide network of "friends" (*nanxin*) to set up daily bureaucratic problems. Government offices are overlapping and often compete with each other. Party-State control is indeed much "cleverer", much more flexible than it used to be. Market mechanisms are more widely understood. Officially the Planning Administration has been over since 1992, but the powerful NDRC (National Development and Reform Commission), which took its place, interferes in any economic decision. Last but not least, in a totalitarian government, the rule of law is by definition meaningless. The corpus of law and regulations is not designed to rule everyone including the State and the Party, but to protect the Party leadership. Legal interpretation is unpredictable and differs from one place to next.

In the economic and financial field, the pyramid of power ranges over three levels: the market is under State control, the State is under the Party control, and the Party … is self-controlled.

Party Leadership

The single Party operates along the standards of "democratic centralism". The economic tenet is the "socialist market economy", whatever it means. Both pairs of terms, "centralism" and "democracy", "market" and "socialism", are not compatible with each other in a Western mind, but they are all consistent "with Chinese characteristics". In Chinese traditional thought, nothing exists without its opposite. This is precisely the interaction of opposite terms that sets things in motion.

Democratic Centralism

CCP is a ruling party that remains, to a certain extent , a revolutionary party, a very secretive and hierarchical one that does not fit with an open and decentralized market economy. The work of the CCP is opaque, not only to average citizens but also to Party members. At each renewal of the leading team (Party Politburo and State Council) every five years, observers from all over the world pack into the People Hall located in Tien An Men square, and scrutinize the icy faces of the seven "elected" members. They have been selected after an opaque procedure within the top spheres of the Party, and are all lined up before a huge picture of the Great Wall. Who is promoted? Who is demoted? Which faction has won the power struggle? Who lost ground?

The 80 Party members are scattered at every single level of the State apparatus and social life: State administrations, State owned companies, all kinds of associations, trade unions, media, churches, non-governmental organizations … down to the block and building party cell. At each level of State administration, a party member supervises the local bureaucrat. Sometimes it is the same person: a province head or town mayor, and the chairman of a State owned company is often also the local party secretary. The Party structure is vertical and hierarchical, which neither facilitates local cooperation between the local Party and State bureaucracy, nor between local offices of each (Party and State) hierarchy.

It has been a long time since the CCP was the advanced guard of the working class made up of the poorest peasants and workers. Since President Jian Ze min's (1989–2002) theory of "double legitimacy", the Party is meant to be a mirror of the whole society. All the business sectors, all of the 53 ethnic minorities, even the 300 million landless and paperless migrants, are represented in the Party Congress. According to the Hurun report (2012) which records the wealthiest people, 360 of the top 1024 richest people were members of the Party Congress. All of them have a combined wealth amounting to $221 billion. The average wealth of each of them was in the range of $1 billion. Most if not all of the heads of the largest State owned and privately owned companies were members of the Central Committee: Wang Jian lin, Chairman of Dalian Wanda Group (owner of American AMC Entertainment and Jurassic Park producer Legendary studios), Lian Wengen, President of Sany Heavy Industries, a manufacturer of public work equipment, Zhou Hai jiang, the owner of a huge textile group, etc. Such membership is not a mere coincidence. The Sany Group plays a key role in China's policy called "infrastructures against raw materials" according to which the commodity producing countries guarantee China's long-term access to the sources of raw materials at market prices. Such sources are desperately needed by the Chinese manufacturing industry. In exchange China takes care of the construction of infrastructure, mostly to connect the pit to the next railway station or sea terminal. Sandy Group is deeply involved in Chinese diplomatic policy, such as the "One belt, one road", the "New Silk Road" policy put forward by President Xi Jin ping such as the creation of development banks such as IIAB (Infrastructure Investment Asian Bank) and NDB (New Development Bank) of the BRICS countries (Brazil, Russia, India, China, South Africa).

The Party is now run like a business venture. Expertise and faithfulness are more important than ideology. Every year Party executives' achievements are assessed by the powerful Organization Department, after a scoring system covering the whole range of business records such as job creation, production and investment growth rates, one child policy, etc. If the Party is attractive to "the best and the brightest" who expect to reach top positions, it is much harder to recruit managers to fulfil the lower levels. Low paid, without the expectation of reaching a higher position, village and small town secretaries use to stay long enough to build up a *nanxin* (i.e. a network of "friends"), all of those for whom they did a favour, but short enough to make it profitable once they have resigned to move to the private sector.

In the past, the CCP leaders were engineers. Now they have an increasing economic and legal education, such as that of the Prime Minister Li Ke qiang. An ambitious Party member cannot reach the highest levels if he is unfamiliar with company management, province government, the chairmanship of a State owned bank or society, or one of the many organizations reporting straight to the State Council. Zhu Qiang, a lawyer, is the secretary of Hebei province (a very sensitive one as Beijing is located in this province); Su Shu lin, former Chairman of Sinopec, a large petro-chemical State owned company, is secretary of the province of Fujian (another sensitive coastal province adjacent to Taiwan island); Sun Zheng cai, who is well known for his research in the agricultural field, is secretary of the Jinlin province, one of the two in Manchuria (in the north east) that include huge oil and coal fields. Before reaching the top, the former Chairman, Hu Jin tao, used to be secretary of the province of Tibet where he was known as a tough leader. Xi Jin ping is a member and former secretary of the Shanghai "gang" (like President Jiang Ze min, Prime Minister Zhu Rong ji and many other top leaders).

Xi Jin ping is meant to be one of the strongest and more powerful leaders. All sources of power are under his control: he is the President of China, secretary of the CCP and Chairman of the Party Military Commission. In reality, he has to make concessions to the Party factions that supported him in reaching the top position. He is not a politician who reached power on the basis of a political programme. His programme is purposely vague and encompassing. No leader can reach the top level unless he is a "reformist", claiming his support of the policy of reform initiated by Deng Xiao ping, 35 years ago. Everyone is more or less "reformist" and in case of a crisis threatening the Party's prominence, some may be more conservative than reformist. To a large extent, the Party secretary is more a referee than the head of government. The collegial way of government is not only a political slogan but a method of governance. The members of the Politburo and the State Council do not necessarily share the same political agenda, but they represent the various factions who share power. The purpose is not to reward followers but to include all of the factions within government in order to prevent opposition from the outside (Fig. 2.1).

Xi Jin ping is perceived as a strong leader because he took a firm stance against dissidents. Actually, he has no choice: the further he wants to promote economic reform, the stronger he should be perceived by the conservatives who are willing to support the reform policy, provided that

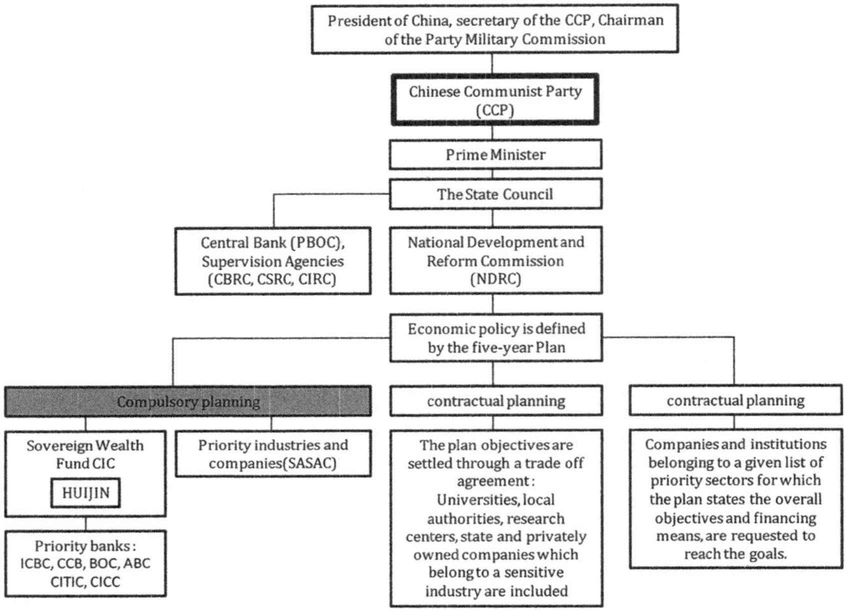

Fig. 2.1 Chinese political and economic organization

the Party rule is unchanged. For Party members, he must guarantee the Party rule; for Chinese citizens, he must guarantee the unwritten covenant that links the Party and the People together—a steady growth of the standard of living against the one Party rule. The ideology shared by Party leaders is a mix of economic reform, political *statu quo* and foreign nationalism.

Socialist Market Economy

Following Mao's death (1976) and Deng Xiao ping's comeback (1978), the policy of reform and opening up was meant to be a new experiment and a new way to socialism, one that was more efficient and more pragmatic. It was not meant to build a capitalist and democratic system. Deng was neither a democrat nor a liberal, but a faithful Communist devoted to his ideal. Several times Party secretary, several times dismissed, every time called back, never eliminated[1] Deng was for years Mao's faithful follower and assistant. He joined the Party when he was 16 and made his career in the wake of Zhou En lai whom he met in France when he was a "student-worker" recruited by contract to fill the position of a French man sent to the trenches. Thanks to his broad and lengthy political, economic and military experience in top positions, he was the obvious and favourite candidate of Party members during the two years of the succession war that followed Mao's death: he guaranteed both economic reform and political *statu quo*.

The policy of reform and opening up is not an ideology; it is not even a political programme. Instead it is a very pragmatic approach to improving the way the Chinese economy works. Among the four "principles" enunciated by Deng Xiao ping, the first and most important one is to maintain and strengthen "the leading role of the Communist Party". The notion of a "socialist market economy" appeared much later in 1992 during the 14th National Congress of the Communist Party. According to the "Chinese" way of doing things, the target is defined after the method, not the other way round. In "*chen*"[2] (zen) though, the archer is going to reach his target provided that he has the proper mindset, regardless of his skill. In the Chinese tradition, the *dao* (the Way) is more important than the goal and the *dao* is going to lead you in the right direction and eventually to the goal. The reform was mentioned in the Constitution in 1993, 15 years later, using ambiguous wording: "the economic planning on the basis of the State ownership". Secretary Jiang Ze min defined the "socialist market economy with Chinese characteristics" under the following items in order of priority: (1) Party leadership, (2) State management, (3) Public ownership, (4) Economic growth, (5) Rural development, (6) Reform of State owned companies and (7) Efficiency and impartiality.[3] The former Prime Minister, Wen Jia bao (2002–2012) defined

---

[1] As opposed to Liu Shao qi, President of the Republic.

[2] "*Chen*" is the chinese word for "*zen*" which was imported from China by the Japanese warriors.

[3] "Party leadership" is the first goal to be mentioned, "efficiency and impartiality" is the last.

the socialist market economy as follows: "The complete formulation of our economic policy consists in leaving the market forces work for the allocation of resources under macro-economic guidance and government regulation."

State Management

The government is not designed to define and implement policy but only to implement the administration's policy defined by the State Council. The highest government body, the State Council, chaired by the Prime Minister, Li Ke qiang, has seven members, each one in charge of a given department. The ministers are not members of the cabinet; they share responsibilities when it comes to policy making though and they are the heads of their respective government administrations. Economic policy is defined by the five-year Plan approved the year before the appointment of the new governing team.

In theory the Plan no longer exists, but actually the five-year Plan stills exists. In 1992 the Planning Office has merely replaces by the NDRC, a powerful body reporting straight to the State Council. The NDRC is in charge of designing the Plan and supervising its implementation. The current Plan is more flexible than the former programme, which was supposed to be a comprehensive one. It combined a volume programme (production, investment, export) with a value "Credit" Plan. However, the NDRC can interfere in any relatively important economic decision such as macro-economic issues like monetary and investment policy, foreign investment, etc. but also in details such as to do with foreign investment projects, interest rates and foreign exchange rates. Each foreign direct investment, each Chinese investment project abroad, each merger and acquisitions of major Chinese companies, etc. are closely scrutinized by the NDRC. Any increase or decrease in the interest rates is set up by the State Council in conjunction with the NDRC and implemented by the central bank.

The category of compulsory planning includes a set of priority industries, banks and companies. The Plan sets up the objectives, the financing resources provided by the central government, the local authorities, and the State owned banks—both commercial banks such as the four State banks (ICBC, CCB, Bank of China, Agricultural Bank of China) and the development banks such as the CDB (China Development Bank) and the China Exim Bank. This includes a number of State owned companies including the 107 groups owned by the government and monitored by the State holding SASAC (State Owned Asset Supervision and Administration Commission) for industrial companies, as well as State banks supervised by Huijin (Central Huijin Investment Co.), a holding company affiliated to the sovereign fund CIC (China Investment Corp.). In addition, all government offices that enjoy a certain level of financial autonomy fall under this category, such as the Ministry of Railways with a total indebtedness of over $3 trillion.[4] The five-year overall Plan is often split down into plans specific to certain areas such as research and development in critical fields (chip manufacturing, solar panels, wind turbines, etc.).

For companies included in this category, the Plan is mandatory. The Plan sets up objectives, financing needs, quantitative targets and qualitative objectives. The State supplies the necessary means in terms of subsidies, bank credit, borrowing from the public, local authority contributions, etc. Sub-plans are elaborated by industry, by region and on an annual basis.

For companies and institutions included in the contractual planning, such as research centres, the plan objectives are settled through a tradeoff agreement: the government commits itself to providing a range of financing such as government and local authority financing in the form of subsidies, tax exemption, bank credit, funds raised from the public, etc. against the completion of certain objectives. In this category all government and other institutions that are granted a certain degree of autonomy, such as universities, local authorities, research centres, State and privately owned companies that belong to a sensitive industry, are included.

In the last category, the contractual one, companies and institutions belonging to a given list of priority sectors for which the Plan states the

[4] Following a corruption scandal (the minister was arrested and convicted of bribery), the Minister of Railway was replaced by an administration reporting to the State Council.

overall objectives and financing means, are requested to reach the goals. Sometimes the overall Plan is split down into economic field, industry sector or companies. Needless to say, although the Plan is not formally compulsory, it is a precondition to tap government financing and State bank credit.

A number of industrial groups, companies, agencies and all kinds of government institutions, are under government control. As a result, overlapping and conflicting interests often occur, and in that case the issue is raised to government level for arbitration. This is the case with all the institutions involved in the financial area such as the central bank, supervision agencies, CBRS for the banking industry, CSRC in the financial markets and CIRC in the insurance industry. In case of persistent conflicts of interest, the government removes the entity concerned from the relevant ministry and makes it report directly to the State Council.

Eventually the government may be constrained to form the so called "leading working groups" specializing in a given area, which unite all the parties involved under the chairmanship of one the members of the State Council. During the 2015 crisis, the government formed a common "leading group", including the central bank and supervisory bodies as well as all the other institutions involved, in order to sort out the obvious lack of cooperation between the two institutions. President Xi Jin ping is said to use the "leading groups" extensively to concentrate power within his hands at the expense of the Prime Minister who is normally in charge of managing economic and financial affairs. The secretary position of each "leading group" is appointed to a Party official close to the Party Secretary. For instance, the secretary position of the "leading group for economic and financial issues", chaired by Xi Jin ping in person, is Liu He, a close associate of the Party Secretary. As a vice-president of the powerful NDRC and head of the Research Department of the State Council, Liu is said to be very influential. He shares the same ideas as the President: he is a devout reformist as well as a strong supporter of the Party rule and a staunch nationalist in foreign affairs, a usual combination in the top spheres of the CCP.

Market Regulation

What is the difference between a "capitalist market economy" and a "socialist market economy"? If the market is a place where offer and demand meet freely in order to determine an equilibrium price that balances both bid and offer, if the market price provides valuable information to consumers who buy, and to entrepreneurs who invest, then the Chinese economy is not a "market economy". As Chen Yun, a veteran and leader of the conservatives during Deng's reign stated: "The market is like the bird in the cage", the "cage" being obviously the Plan. The European Union's decision to give the status of "market economy" to China as well as the IMF's decision to select the yuan among the currencies (US$, Euro, yen, sterling) included in the SDR (Special Drawing Rights) are entirely political without any economic ground. According to the 2001 WTO (World Trade Organization) treaty of China's membership, the USA and the European Union should give China the status of a "market economy" to lift the last trade barriers, but both of them are reluctant to do so on the grounds that the "market economy with Chinese characteristics" is far from a standard market economy.[5]

Property Right

In China property right is acknowledged by the 1982 Constitution and in theory protected by law. Most of the State owned companies are inherited from the times of the planned economy and belong to the industrial sectors that the government sees as strategic. A number of huge private groups are big enough to be closely looked after by the government. These include most of the big privately owned companies, such as internet companies, that have emerged in the new (digital) economy or industries that the government sees as less strategic, such as the real estate business, even though they are nonetheless

[5] As a result of the Brexit vote, China has lost the UK as a strong supporter of granting China the status of a market economy by the European Union.

under government control. Some of the industries that used to be marginal have moved into the very heart of the government's industrial policy, such as the chip manufacturing industry. A development plan was approved in 2016 in this area to lower China's dependency on Taiwanese, Korean and US imports. A number of high-tech companies are actually former research centres linked to academies of science or prominent universities such as Tsinghua University (Beijing) and Fudan University (Shanghaî). A research department was first disconnected as a company and eventually removed as a full-fledged company, such as Lenovo, the world's largest PC company that acquired IBM PC's department in 2005.

The actual legal statute does not make a difference between State owned and privately owned companies. A great number of Chinese companies include State owned companies, government institutions or local authorities among their shareholders: sovereign funds such as CIC, development banks such CDB, pension funds such as NSSF (National Social Security Fund), State owned companies affiliated to SASAC for industrial companies, or Huijin (Central Huijin Investment) for State banks and China Investment and Trust Co. (CITIC) for financial companies. It is prohibited for State owned banks (ICBC, CCB, BOC, ABC, BOCOM) to acquire industrial companies with customer deposits. However, in 2016, the government authorized State banks to swap the non-performing loans extended to defaulting companies against stocks (a measure that did not improve companies' management and kept alive "zombie" companies, but one that decreased the lending banks' rights in case of default, triggering a crisis in the banking industry). Whatever the legal status is, and no matter who the shareholders are, private or public companies are closely supervised by the Party-State.

The privatization process is not aimed at transferring ownership to private shareholders but only to submit the "privatized" companies to "market discipline" in terms of profitability, information and competition. It is also a way to widen sources of financing by tapping the huge public savings through financial markets. It is expected to be the best way to improve companies' management while keeping companies under control.

The government holding SASAC oversees 106 manufacturing companies (December 2015). State owned companies enjoy a monopoly situation, unlimited access to bank credit from State banks, government subsidies and financing, low or no dividend payments, tax exemption, etc. In 2014 the government issued a decree providing that State owned companies should produce a 5% return on equity and pay dividends to the State.

The direct or indirect State owned companies exist in a number of critical sectors such as the nuclear industry (CNNC, China National Nuclear Corp. which has joined Areva to build Hinkley nuclear power plant and is going to build three nuclear power plants in Argentina including two China-made fourth-generation ones), power production (China Power Industrial Corp., Harbin Electric Corp., Dongfang Electric Corp.), distribution networks (China Southern Power Grid), aerospace (China Aerospace Science and Technological Corp.), aircraft (AVIC, Aviation Industry Corp. that is about to launch the first China-made aircraft C909), shipyards (China Shipbuilding Industry Corp., China State Shipbuilding Corp.), the petroleum industry, both production (CNPC, China National Petroleum Corp., the holding company of Petrochina), and distribution (Sinopec), chemicals (Sinochem), telecommunications (China Mobile, China Unicom, China Telecommunications, the last two being merged shortly), car industry (Donfeng that took a 30% share in Peugeot), steel (Baosteel, Anshan Iron & Steel Group, Wuhan Iron & Steel Corp.), airways (China Eastern Airlines Corp., China Southern Air Holding, China Aviation Holding Cy.), shipping (COSCO, China Ocean Shipping Cy. that owns and run the Pireus terminals), seeds and fertilizers (ChemChina that acquired the large Swiss agro-business Syngenta in 2016), and so on.

In the banking and financial industry, Huijin owns or holds a majority share in the four State banks (ICBC, CCB, BOC, ABC), which accounts for half of the total bank credit, policy banks (CDB), investment banks (CITIC), commercial banks (China Everbright, China Merchant Bank), insurance companies (China Reinsurance, Ping An, China Life, Anbang that is bidding for the US hotel chain, Starwood), investment funds (China Jianyin Investment, China Galaxy Financial Holding), and securities trading companies (Shenyin & Wanguo Securities, Guotai Securities, Guofen Securities).

Last but not least, thousands of regional banks and companies from a wide spectrum of industries are wholly or partially owned and managed by local governments.

Rule of Law

In China a company involved in a lawsuit should have a good network of relationships (*nanxin*) rather than rely upon the courts. The law may be understood in different ways according to the court. It is the same Minister who supervises courts, police and security. The Party has a network of legal offices scattered all over the country, in every jurisdiction, in charge of supervising judges and lawyers. Prior to referring a matter to court, the judge checks with the local Party legal office as to whether or not he is competent. Prior to the final decision, he asks for advice from the local Party legal office to make sure that his interpretation of the law is correct. If a sensitive issue, for instance a claim involving a Party member, is referred to him then he states that he is not competent and the case is transferred to the Party. The Party has its own courts and jails. Someone may be caught by Party officials and detained without notice for an unlimited period of time. A number of high-ranking officials and prominent businessmen have disappeared; some of them have shown up after a while without further explanation.

A legal case is often a way to wipe out a competitor, especially if it is a foreigner, or even worse Japanese. A number of foreign companies have already experienced the "fairness" of Chinese courts at their expense. In 1987, the French dairy group Danone formed a joint venture with the Chinese group Wahaha, a beverage company owned by Zong Qing hou, one of the richest men in China known to be close to the Party, to market its products all over China. In 1997, Danone and Wahaha formed five joint ventures for the marketing of Danone products in China. Ten years later, Danone realized that several companies from the Wahaha group were selling Danone products under their own brands. After a lengthy procedure that lasted several years, Danone, which was claiming $3 billion in damages, was eventually sentenced to pay $250 million to Wahaha for breaching patent rights that in the meantime had become unexpectedly "Chinese" and Wahaha's property.

The Party-State keeps a tight control over banks, public and private companies, and markets. Party-State influence extends over State owned companies and banks, through a wide range of instruments. The government's control fits with government objectives. The more sensitive the industry or the company, the tighter government control is. In the areas that are meant to be less sensitive, the government uses more flexible instruments, which are more suitable for letting market mechanisms work, while keeping a tight control over the most sensitive companies and industries.

In China, politics and economics are tightly connected. The government interferes with market mechanisms so that the market cannot fulfil its functions: not only to set a free price, but also to provide reliable information to consumers and producers. China is neither a market economy nor a capitalist one; not even a State capitalist one. In China, not only banks and companies, but the market itself, are under State control.

3

A Non-Independent Central Bank

Today all the central banks of developed countries are independent from the government. The notion of central bank independence is based on economic and financial motives, but above all it is tightly linked to the democratic system: the checks and balances system of power. Like courts and the press, the central bank is a magistrate in its own field and as such it is expected to be free from the other power centres. As the court is in charge of law enforcement, so the central bank is in charge of price and financial stability. Price stability (i.e. the domestic value of money) being a public good, the central bank has a duty to act as a counter-power and make sure that monetary policy is implemented free of government interference. In China the mere idea of an independent centre of power from the Party-State is not compatible with the Chinese communist regime, nor with the multi-century history and political tradition of China: central power could be delegated but not decentralized. For centuries, due to the huge size of its territory and population, China has been centralized, broken down and reunited again and again. Centralization is a basic feature of Chinese politics. From this perspective, Mao was the last in a long line beginning with the first emperor, Shi Huang di, who united China in 220 BC through blood and violence. As opposed to Western empires, the Chinese Empire

D. De Rambures, F. Escobar Duenas, *China's Financial System*,
DOI 10.1007/978-3-319-40451-6_3

has never experienced any form of feudalism, i.e. a hereditary power handed over to a local baron over a given territory and population. By definition, local power is limited in time and may be cancelled at any time.

Deng Xiao ping has always expressed a strong distrust of the political system of checks and balances. It was not so much an ideological posture but a pragmatic one. He thought that not only was the multi-party system incompatible with the Chinese political tradition, but above all, it was incompatible with the policy of reform and opening up. In order to implement a difficult transition from the planned economy to a more flexible and decentralized one, China needed a strong and highly centralized system of government.

Central Bank Independence

According to Keynesian though, there is a given mix of interest rate, exchange rate and budget deficit that is compatible with full employment and price stability. In a system of floating exchange rates, the exchange rate is neutralized. Consequently successful growth policy, full employment and price stability depend on the mix between budget deficit and interest rate, between fiscal and monetary policy. Therefore, the two policies should be implemented by two independent yet cooperating bodies.

In the post-war period, priority was given to reconstruction and full employment, and hence a certain level of inflation was tolerated. In the 1970s, following the surge of oil prices, priority shifted towards the fight against inflation. As "*inflation is always and everywhere a monetary phenomenon*",[1] the fight against inflationary pressure should be handled by an independent central bank to offset a permissible fiscal policy and prevent the excessive supply of money through a budget deficit. In the aftermath of the 2008 crisis, in the context of deepening recession and growing unemployment, it may be debatable that such a critical power is committed to an independent body without democratic mandate. In addition, to fulfil its function, central banks resorted to new techniques under the guise of "quantitative easing" (buying government bonds and later corporate bonds)

[1] As Milton Friedmann and Anna Schwartz wrote an influential book, *A Monetary History of the United States, 1867–1960.*

far beyond their constitutional boundaries. The world crisis, the worst one since the 1930s, entailed a return of the State to the main stage.

In this perspective, the highly centralized Chinese political system was to some extent ahead of other countries. China's central government reacted much faster and more strongly than any other country; faster than the USA in the election year and much faster than the European Union. It combined the whole range of available instruments: government subsidies, bank loans, tax exemptions and salary rises. Several recovery plans were implemented in the following years. Eventually the global crisis hit the Chinese economy as well. The slowing down of the Chinese economy is due to a combination of two factors: a short-term one, i.e. the decrease in foreign (mostly Western) demand; and a longer-term one, i.e. the transition process to a new economy focusing on household consumption, service industries and innovation.

China's Central Bank Statute

Although China's central bank, the PBOC (People's Bank of China), is in charge of monetary policy and allocates all the necessary tools, monetary policy is defined by the State Council. All major decisions (interest rates, exchange rates, reserve requirements, open market policies) are taken by the State Council and implemented by the central bank. As a result, all or most of the key decisions are taken on political grounds rather than economic ones. But the split between "political" and "economic" spheres is meaningless in China. The central bank's duty is to implement the policy designed, and the decisions taken, by the State Council.

The central bank statute is based upon two laws: the 1984 law removed the central bank from the Ministry of Finance's control to be transferred under the direct control of the State Council, ensuring its administrative "independence"; and the 1995 law that formally guarantees the Central Bank's "independence". Article 7 of the 1995 law provides that "*the PBOC is free from any interference from local governments, administrative bodies at any level and public or private organizations*". Actually the law refers to a usual practice of local government: it is quite difficult for a local central bank officer to turn down a request from the local Party secretary. This has nothing to do with central bank independence as it is understood in Western countries.

Article 2 of the 1995 law is more specific: "*PBOC defines and puts in force the monetary policies (in plural), implements oversight and control over the financial sector under the supervision of the State Council.*" According to Article 3, the aim of monetary policies is "*to ensure the stability of the value of money and to stimulate economic growth*". According to the law, the central bank is in charge of the domestic value of money (price stability) and foreign value (exchange rate). The objectives of the PBOC mandate are wider than the ECB's (European Central Bank's) restricted mandate, limited to price and financial stability, but narrower than the Fed's one, which is extended to economic growth and full employment.

The PBOC's influence within the Party apparatus and the Chinese decision making system is owed to the growing role of monetary and exchange policy in the management of economic policy and the transition of the economic system towards some form of more decentralized market economy. The Central bank and its governor, the charismatic and influential Zhu Xiao chuan, are said to be more favourable to the implementation of market mechanisms than the Ministry of Finance. Actually this appears to be more like a form of division of labour between the two institutions. The State Council is leaning towards one or the other according to the circumstances and the necessary balance between the Party factions.

The most sensitive reforms are implemented in a well-organized manner: a high-ranking official other than a member of the Politburo or the State Council, who does not involve the Party or the State, puts forward a proposal. According to the way the lower levels of the Party react, the proposal is taken over by the government for implementation at a local level and then at a national one, or dropped.

Zhu Xiao chuan, technician and reformist

Zhu Xiao chuan has been Chairman of the PBOC since 2002: an achievement in the Chinese political system that usually requires all top positions to be renewed every five years. Zhu Xiao chuan has worked with three Party secretaries (Jiang Ze min, Hu Jin tao and Xi Jin ping). A prominent member of the "Shanghai gang" and a "princeling" (*taizi*) like Xi Jin ping, Zhu Xiao chuan is perceived as

(*continued*)

(continued)

a technician and a pro-marketer, favourable to market mechanisms regulating the Chinese economy.

Zhu's father, Zhu Jian nan, was a prominent member of the secret services and Minister of Industry. Like Xi Jin ping's father, Zhu Jian nan was a victim of the witch-hunt during the Cultural Revolution. But unlike Xi Jin ping who was sent for 10 years to a remote and poor province, Zhu junior was the head of a brigade of Red Guards, and selected as a member of the "poor peasant and worker class" to join the prestigious Beijing-based Tsinghua University. Initially Zhu was close to Zhao Zi yang, then he became Prime Minister and later Party Secretary, appointed by Deng Xiao ping to implement the policy of reforms. Zhao was eliminated during the May–June 1989 Tien An Men events because he was supporting a more flexible approach to sorting out the student uprising. Zhao was replaced by Jiang Ze min, who became Shanghai's Party secretary, and is former protégé of Zhu senior who helped him build his career. Zhu Xiao chuan joined the bandwagon and rallied the new leader, Jiang Ze min.

Zhu is a technician with lengthy experience. He was the head of the SAFE (State Agency for Foreign Exchange), the powerful PBOC's department in charge of managing foreign exchange reserves, then Chairman of the CCB (China Construction Bank), one of the four State banks. He reshaped the CCB to become a successful commercial bank by transferring non-performing loans to a defeasance company, AMC (Asset Management Cy.) called "Cinda", and finally became Chairman of the CSRC (China Securities Regulatory Commission), the supervisory body of the financial markets. Zhu married Li Ling, head of the legal department of the Ministry of Commerce, who has been involved in the negotiation of China's treaty membership of the WTO (World Trade Organization).

As opposed to Chinese tradition, Zhu was appointed by Jiang Ze min in 2002, a post renewed by Hu Jin tao in 2003 and Xi Jin ping in 2012. This is evidence of his personal skills, but also of the growing influence of monetary and exchange policy in China's economic policy.

Central Bank Functions

Like the other central banks, the PBOC fulfils three basic functions: the management of the interbank payment system, monetary policy and supervision of the banking sector.

The Management of the Interbank Payment System

In a market economy, the interbank payment system plays a key role in the implementation of monetary policy. The interbank market is the locus where all payments are centralized and settled. It is both a source of information to the central bank and the place where the central bank finalizes interbank payments and regulates the money supply, to provide additional cash to banks if and when needed, or to absorb excess cash. In China, the smooth working of the interbank payment system is of particular importance in view of the size of the country. China has one time zone all over the territory, which in fact stretches over five time zones.

From 2002 onwards, the PBOC has been using a RTGS (Real Time Gross Settlement System) interbank payment system which clears and settles high-value payment orders (HPVS: High Value Payment System) issued by banks. PBOC uses the CNAPS (China National Advanced Payment System) computer and telecommunication system for the whole process: transmission, clearing and settlement in real time of payment orders channelled from all over the country. Since then, the PBOC has kept improving the system which has been extended to all sorts of payment instruments (small amounts, credit cards) and all the markets other than cash payment (stock exchange). The Chinese exchange markets use a DVP (Delivery Versus Payment) system which connects both the cash market and the security market to make sure that the two legs of the transaction are completed on a simultaneous basis.

Until recently, credit card networks, including the foreign ones (Visa, Mastercard), were constrained to settling payments through the official Chinese clearing system (UniPay) created by the PBOC, then removed from the central bank's control to be transferred to a "private" company owned and operated by the four State banks (ICBC, CCB, BOC, ABC). In 2015 Visa and Mastercard were allowed to use their own clearing system, but at this time Unipay had already captured 80% of the market share. In addition the PBOC has imposed the PBOC 3.0 standards on foreign networks instead of the EM (Europay) standards used by Visa and Mastercard. As a result all plastic cards have had to be remade. If foreign credit card networks make a claim to the WTO they have a good chance of winning after several years of legal proceedings, but in the meantime they would lose the Chinese market.

In most Western countries, all the interbank payments are cleared and settled through two types of network—one "public" managed by the central bank, and one "private" managed by the banks themselves—even though all the payments are eventually settled in central money, i.e. through the bank accounts with the central bank (central money): Fedwire and CHIPS in the USA, TARGET and EBA in the euro zone, CHAPS and BACS in the UK. The aim is to maintain a certain level of competition between both payment systems in terms of fees, delays of payment and other services. Although fees in the Chinese interbank payment system are set at cost price, there is only one payment system so far.

Monetary Policy

The efficiency of monetary policy is measured with a given set of objectives (interest rates, money supply) achieved with the minimum amount of cash and the shortest delay in transmission. The market capacity of spreading interest rate movements and the cash injection to the whole economy depends upon the efficiency of the transmission mechanism: to get the maximum effect while using the minimum means possible. In addition to the usual set of market instruments—interest rates, reserve requirements, open market transactions—the PBOC can use quantitative instruments such as lending quotas, and can even resort to quite unusual and more stringent measures such as police enquiry, detention and lawsuits if the previous ones proved to be insufficient.

Market Instruments

In order to reach the target rate of interest without disturbing the interbank cash market, central banks combine a mix of price (borrowing rates of the banks) and quantity (reserve requirement, i.e. the compulsory bank deposit with the central bank). With the bank borrowing rate, the central bank is expected to spread the interest rate change over the whole economy. With the reserve requirement, the central bank is expected to increase or decrease market liquidity and to shrink or expand the volume of lending.

To prevent financial bias caused by the sudden implementation of such measures, the central bank can resort to open market transactions. Through buying or selling short-term treasury and government bonds, the central bank resorts to a far more flexible and efficient way of regulating both the price and the volume of money supply. This is provided of course that an efficient interbank cash market (deep and broad) exists to reach the maximum result with the minimum amount of cash.

China's $7 trillion Treasury bond market is indeed large enough to accommodate any open market transaction initiated by the central bank. However, for a number of reasons, the transmission mechanism does not work as it should. Bank rates do not apply to the entire economy. A number of potential borrowers who have no access to bank loans have to turn to informal credit, which is beyond the central bank's control. These borrowers include small companies, private companies, service companies that have no collateral available, and high-tech companies that have no capital base and are not strong enough. Most of the bank's lending capacity, and to begin with State banks', is restricted to State owned companies. The interest rate moves are not passed on to the final borrowers, as all the most prominent borrowing companies are meant to be supported by explicit or implicit State guarantees. Finally, all banks prefer to hold the cash available on their accounts with the central bank (free reserve) rather than to relend to other banks on the interbank money market. In case of credit shrinkage, increased borrowing cost through refinancing from the central bank or an increase in reserve requirement, commercial banks are going to draw on the free reserves of the central bank (in excess of the required deposits).

Quantitative and Administrative Measures

From the times of a planned economy, the PBOC has inherited a wide range of quantitative instruments such as credit quotas and lending limits. Within the framework of the 2008 recovery plan, the PBOC dispatched instructions to commercial banks to increase the volume of loans granted. In addition to $600 billion government subsidies, banks extended twice as much credit ($1600 billion) in 2009 as in the year before. As a result, a huge number of loans has been wasted in useless infrastructure projects, industrial over-capacities, or misdirected to finance the purchase of securities. Banks may be required to increase (or decrease) lending in some specific areas: internal provinces rather than the well-off coastal provinces, rural and agricultural firms, small and medium-sized enterprises (SMEs) and real estate. Accounting for more than 20% of GDP, the real estate business can boost growth in a variety of industrial sectors: construction, public works, cement, steel, and glass.

Window Guidance

The "Window Guidance" policy is drawn from the Japanese experience of the 1990s to make sure that government directives regarding credit policy are duly implemented by commercial banks as planned. In every Chinese bank, a "compliance department" is in touch with the central bank in order not only to make sure that government instructions are implemented, but if necessary to interfere with a given loan or the restructuring plan of a defaulting company.

In 2007, on the eve of the financial crisis, while consumer prices were growing fast, the government used the window guidance channel to induce banks to extend loans to the pork producers (pork is a basic Chinese food) with the aim of curbing the price increase. In 2009, as the financial crisis reached its apex, while the government was attempting to keep control over bank credit, the CBRC, the bank supervision authority, dispatched a circular "notice" (*Real Estate Market and Capital Market* notice) to eleven banks instructing them to lower the volume of lending to the financing of real estate and the purchase of securities as a way to cool down the fast-growing industries while avoiding hindering the recovery in process. In June 2012, the CBRC sent a "secret" circular letter to the banks in which it requested banks to limit steel industry lending, because the proceeds were being used to speculate on raw material (coal, iron) markets.

Interest Rate Liberalization

Until recently the PBOC used to fix the bank interest rate, both the interest paid to the bank deposit and saving accounts, and the interest charged to the borrower, so that the gross bank margin was guaranteed. The interest rate paid on a one-year deposit was capped at 3% ± 10% of 3% (i.e. 3.3%) and the interest charged to the borrowers was capped at 6% ± 30% of 6% (i.e. 8%), ensuring a 3% plus gross margin to banks. Over the last few years, the PBOC has not changed or cancelled the system, but allowed the banks to market new saving instruments. The aim was to strengthen competition by designing new saving schemes to increase the rate offered to customers. Wealth Management Products (WMPs) are synthetic products that include several slices of credit in a single security, quite similar to the well-known sub-primes. The "trust" is an investment company buying loans from banks. This is a very appealing investment product for both the customer and the bank. For the customer, it is an opportunity to get a much higher return (6–8% and more) than with a bank saving account. For the bank, it is a way of selling assets from its loan portfolio and rebuilding its lending capacity. In most cases, the trust company is formed at the initiative of the bank, as a way to get rid of the potential problematic loans. To customers, it is a very risky investment as they do not know what the nature of the claims acquired by the trust company is and, in case of default, they have no recourse against the issuing bank.

On the lending side, the rate of liberalization has not reached its goal as banks did not increase their lending to SMEs, which are mostly private companies, on the grounds that such companies do not have reliable accounting practices and do not hold fixed assets as collateral. As a result, the State banks and most of the commercial banks have restricted their lending to State owned companies and local governments, which are granted a *de facto* guarantee from the State.

Supervision

Bank supervision is shared between the central bank (PBOC) and the State regulation agency (CBRC). In theory, the field of each institution is well defined: the central bank deals with monetary policy and financial stability whereas the supervision body deals with regulation and control over the banks. The central bank is in charge of financial stability, including bank solvency and market liquidity. Without it no monetary policy is possible. The central bank sets up the liquidity and capital ratios of the banks. The CBRC is in charge of designing and implementing the banking regulations. Indeed, the CBRC controls access to the banking industry, granting banking licences at the national, provincial or city level according to the geographic extent of the banking licence.

The implementation of monetary policy demands close cooperation between the two institutions and a procedure for sorting out the inevitable conflicts of interest between the two government bodies. The Chairman of the PBOC is a member of the board of the CBRC and, vice versa, the head of the CBRC is a member of the monetary committee of the central bank. As a last resort, the two institutions report directly to the State Council which acts as a referee in cases of conflict. Following the 2015 stock exchange and foreign exchange crisis, the State Council formed a special ad hoc committee made up of all the parties involved under the chairmanship of the Prime Minister. Such a decision making scheme is obvious in a very centralized system based on hierarchical links and does not rely on cross links designed to settle cooperation problems between institutions at the same level. Consequently, most of the policy issues are settled on political grounds rather than on technical ones.

As the body in charge of stability and soundness of the banking industry, the central bank is in charge of setting up bank ratios, but the supervision agency (CBRC) is in charge of implementing the Basel standards regarding capital ratios. In July 2013, the PBOC removed the ceiling rate which used to prohibit banks from lending at a rate lower than the fixed rate (then 6%), by more than 30% (4%). In July 2013, the PBOC forbade banks to pay 10% above the fixed rate (then 3%). In July 2014, a joint directive from the PBOC and the CBRC has somewhat softened the lending ratio. The banking regulation provides that the banks are not allowed to lend more than 75% of their total deposits. The new regulation did not change this provision, but ensured that the loan categories which are included in the computation of the ratio have been reduced while the definition of the deposit included in the computation of the deposit base was increased. But it was the PBOC alone that removed from the 75% lending ratio the loans to SMEs (which account for two-thirds of the growth rate, 60% of GDP, 50% of the fiscal resources and 80% of urban jobs) in the expectation of directing available credit to the sectors that most needed it.

The two institutions, PBOC and CBRC, are said to have divergent approaches to the transition process. The central bank and its governor, Zhu Xiao chuan, rely upon market mechanisms, while the supervision agency and its former head, Liu Min, are prone to State control. The two men are close to each other as far as their education and careers are concerned, but they belong to different racing stables.

Both were appointed at the same time, in 2002, with Zhu as Chairman of the central bank, and Liu as head of the newly formed CBRC, until he was replaced in 2011 by Shang Fu li. Zhu is an engineer who graduated in computer science, a very useful background for implementing the new payment system and new financial techniques. Liu and Shang have a strong grounding in economic and financial matters. Both of them have served in high-ranking provincial positions: Zhu was Party secretary of Shanghai; Liu Party secretary of Fujian, a very sensitive position given its proximity to Taiwan. Both of them have chaired big State banks: Zhu as Chairman of CCB, Shang as Chairman of ABC. Shang took over Zhu's position as head of the CSRC before he was appointed head of the CBRC. The three of them (Zhu, Liu, Shang) used to be members of the Central Committee, but none of them have been members of the top positions, in the Party Politburo or the State Council. However, Zhu is a more political animal. Zhu used to be head of the SAFE, the central bank department in charge of the management of foreign exchange reserves. He was also a member of the powerful NDRC, the body which succeeded the Plan and is involved in any economic and financial decision of importance. Zhu is perceived as more inclined to let the market mechanisms work: "If the market can solve a problem, let us work the market forces. I am only a referee, not a coach."

Crisis Management

During the week of 10–15 June 2013, the borrowing cost of the two sources of cash to level the bank's cash position (overnight, seven-day repos) blew up. The overnight interest rates which used to fluctuate within a 2–3% bracket, jumped up to 9.6%, and the seven-day repo rose from 3% to 12%. On 20 June, interest rates on the interbank money market reached 20%. Later on the market realized that China's Everbright Bank (a commercial bank affiliated to a State wholly owned financial group) had defaulted.

While the government was wondering what to do next, the crisis was spreading quickly to the credit and exchange markets. The Shanghai Stock Exchange lost 10% in one day and 15% in one month. Investors could not get credit to buy stocks. The stock markets kept falling. China's Agricultural Bank, which was about to launch an IPO (Initial Public Offering), was instructed to postpone the transaction. Banks stopped granting credit, did not renew outstanding loans and increased interest rates charged to customers. The banks that depended on the interbank money market for refinancing passed the rate increase on to their customers' borrowings. Most of the commercial banks, which had a much lower borrowing cost thanks to their customer deposit base and other sources of funds, took this opportunity to increase the interest rates charged to customer loans nonetheless. The money market was soon hit by the crisis. As they could not raise funds from the market, banks that had a short position (borrowers) turned to the central bank to get the financing needed to square their daily position with the central bank. Also, banks with a long position (lenders) turned to the central bank to invest their excess funds, as they did not trust the other banks' solvency. As a result the interbank money market was frozen and does not function any more.

While the members of the State Council were debating about the right solution, the crisis was spreading rapidly to the rest of the economy: the money market was blocked, the credit market was frozen and financial markets dropped. Actually the crisis was mostly due to government policy. In the aftermath of the 2008 financial crisis, the government had poured over $2 trillion in total into the economy (central government subsidies, local government contributions, bank loans). As the Chinese economy was bouncing back, the government tried to call back the excess liquidity which was flooding the markets as a result of the increase in bank borrowing rates and the bank reserve requirement combined with open market transactions. In spite of these measures, the volume of credit kept growing. The indebtedness of the whole economy was twice as much as a year before: 207% of GDP by the end of 2013 as opposed to 107% by the end of 2011. Some companies that could not get new loans from banks turned to new types of credit to pay suppliers. The volume of bank acceptances reached Rmb 6 trillion ($1 trillion) by the end of 2012 following a rise of 22% in 2012 and 21% in 2011. Unable to get credit from banks, a number of companies turned to the black market (informal credit) which is beyond the central bank's control. In such a context it was inevitable that a liquidity crisis would blow up sooner or later, a crisis made worse by the inability of the market to fulfil its function of collecting funds from the banks with an excess and directing the excess to those who desperately needed it.

Initially the central bank attributed the crisis to the banks that had reached or overcame their lending quotas (up to 75% of their deposit base) and could not raise funds from the market. Once refinancing was granted to the near defaulting banks, the market would get back to normal. The *People's Daily*, the Party's newspaper, stated that "*the PBOC (the central bank) is not the* 'milk cow' *of banks*". The media were instructed by the Party to avoid such sentences as "the so called liquidity crisis" and to state that the markets were properly supplied. As the crisis deepened, the PBOC jumped into the battlefield. Fifteen days after the crisis blew up, Rmb 17 billion ($2.7 billion) was injected into the market in one day (Monday 13 June). Later on, the PBOC stated that the intervention delay was a deliberate warning to banks to improve their cash management.

The consequences of the cash shrinkage are still felt today. Banks, either in short or long positions, turned to the central bank rather than to the interbank market. Borrowing banks switched to the central bank for refinancing. Lending banks increased their free reserves with the central bank. The money market could not work and the central bank's monetary policy was losing efficiency. In addition, the central bank had a communication problem with the market, a critical issue in such circumstances. At that very moment, the market was expecting a strong statement from the central bank, while the Party Politburo and the State Council kept debating as the crisis was deepening.

On the other hand, the government was bailing out defaulting banks and state companies to avoid a wave of bankruptcies, dragging the whole market behind. As both investors and managers were fully convinced that the government would intervene in cases of default by a bank or company, there was no moral hazard for investors. In actual fact, the State was acting as the lender of last resort.

In a market economy the credit system is built on a pyramid-shaped scheme: as household debt is not negotiable (except in sub-prime types of securities), they are taken over by companies (consumer credit, real estate loans); as companies' claims (such as delays of payment) are not easily negotiable, except for the happy few who are big enough to tap the market directly, they are taken over by banks (against a discount); as bank claims in times of crisis are not easily tradable, they are transferred to the central bank's balance sheet; and in the event of a cash crisis spreading, the bank claims are taken over by the State. In China the market does not work as it should, so eventually all the claims move up to State level.

4

Chinese Banks: Between Control and Profitability

The banking and financial sector has been the last one to be dealt with in the agenda of reform policy and opening up. The financial system plays a critical role in the management of the economy, but the challenge is less economic than political. Banking reform raises a lot of political arguments among Party members, between reformists and conservatives, pro-marketers and pro-statists, between those supporting a further opening and those reluctant to lower the barriers. No doubt it was much easier to cope with the people's communes and State owned companies rather than the financial markets which had to be designed and implemented from scratch.

In China, all types of banking and financial institutions that are needed in a market economy exist, but the banking sector is closely linked to the State, whether it is owned or tightly controlled by the government, or both. The banks and financial institutions are not designed to make a profit but to implement the Plan and the Party's directives. Profitability is requested but it is not a primary concern. Profit is only a sign of good management, but this is arguable to the extent that most of the input is highly dependent on Party and State influence. Some factors are free,

D. De Rambures, F. Escobar Duenas, *China's Financial System*,
DOI 10.1007/978-3-319-40451-6_4

some are not, and it is hard to know which one contributes most to profit making. How much is owed to management, to regulation, to the monopoly situation, to the State's ownership?

The State as a Regulator

The controlling agency is the CBRC (China Banking Regulatory Commission) created in 2003 under a law on bank regulation and supervision. According to Article 1 of the law, the CBRC is in charge of "*ensuring the protection of the depositors and consumers, [and to] promote the competitiveness of the Chinese banking industry, [and to] promote economic and social development*". On this basis, CBRC regulation is involved on a much wider scale.

In Article 2, are listed the fields which fall within CBRC authority: banking institutions, the content of the banking business, the banking products and services, the supply of information, and education of the public. Article 21 focuses on the CBRC's prudential regulation: capital ratio, quality of loans, amortization of non-performing loans, risk concentration and liquidity management. The law makes a distinction between short-, medium- and long-term objectives. In the short term, the CBRC must "*establish prudential regulation*". In the medium term, the CBRC must "*strengthen risk supervision; set up legal and regulation framework to adapt the banking industry to a more open environment, to prevent financial risks and ensure security of transactions*". In the long term the CBRC must "*improve the market of banking institutions, ensure security of banking transactions and improve competitiveness of the Chinese financial market*". The legal objectives of the CBRC put emphasis on the stability of the market (regulation, prudential rules, risk supervision) and the competitiveness of banks (through increased competition).

New banking products and services must be authorized by the CBRC and each application is screened on a case by case basis. Since 2015, the CBRC's authority has been restricted to checking whether new products and services are in compliance with legal and regulatory provisions. In practice, nothing seems to have changed so far.

PBOC versus CBRC

The 2003 law (Article 9) provided that it is up to the State Council to arbitrate between the two institutions, but Article 35 of the same law provided that the two institutions should set up some sort of system for sharing information. However, nothing of that sort seems to be in operation yet as in the aftermath of the 2015 crisis the State Council was forced to create an ad hoc working committee including all the parties involved. According to the "Peter principle",[1] the final word is raised to the first level of incompetence.

According to the law, the central bank is in charge of prudential regulation. However, in April 2004, with the aim of circumscribing its territory, the CBRC issued a directive requesting banks to restrict credit growth "*without the central bank's authorization*". Once again in 2007, the CBRC defined the banks' capital ratio and performed stress tests which fall within the central bank's duties (*Guidance on Commercial Banks Stress Tests*).

In order to increase lending to small companies in line with the Plan guidelines, the CBRC requested, in June 2011, that the loans extended to small and medium-sized enterprises (SMEs) should be withdrawn from the computation of the lending ratio according to which bank loans should not exceed 75% of the deposit base (*Note Concerning Improving Financial Services to Small Entities*). In the meantime, the People's Bank of China (PBOC) implemented credit restrictions to limit the growth of bank lending. The bank's reserve requirement was increased by 0.5%. In June 2012 the PBOC dictated that the ratio of disbursed loans to credit commitments should not exceed 80%. Both decisions were not consistent: due to the credit restrictions imposed by the central bank, banks had no more room within their credit ceiling to allocate to small companies, as planned by the CBRC.

Until recently, there was no deposit guarantee regulation, but both institutions have been competing/cooperating to put forward a new deposit insurance scheme. In 2004, the PBOC issued a draft paper about a system of deposit guarantee drawn from the American FDIC.[2]

[1] *The Peter Principle* (1968) by Laurence J. Peter (1919–1990).

[2] Federal Deposit Insurance Corp. created in 1933 to cope with the wave of bank failures during the Great Depression.

In 2008 a common report by the PBOC and CBRC to the State Council (*Request of the People's Bank of China and the China Banking Regulatory Commission on Instructions for the Implementation Plan of China's Deposit Insurance Mechanism*) was approved by the State Council but not implemented because it needed a decision about which organization would be overseeing the new system. In 2012 the CBRC formed a Consumers' Protection Bureau to collect customers' claims. The same year, the PBOC set up a Financial Consumer Protection Bureau. Then the CBRC issued several documents relating to savers' protection: "*Outline of Consumer Works in the Banking Sector*" (2012–2015), "*Key Issues in Consumer Works in the Banking Sector*" (2013) while the PBOC issued "*Rules on Financial Consumer Protection Works*". Eventually, a deposit insurance scheme became operational from May 2015. The Chinese Deposit Insurance Scheme guarantees deposits up to Rmb 500,000 ($81,000) which according to the CBRC covers 99.6% of all depositors, but does not mention how much out of the total $18.2 trillion deposit base (the world's largest) is covered. As a matter of comparison, following the 2008 banking crisis, the American FDIC deposit guarantee was raised from $100,000 to $200,000.

However, in some areas the PBOC and CBRC have managed to cooperate. In 2011 a joint directive signed by both institutions was issued to restructure compulsory banking fees (*Notice Concerning Financial Institutions Charging Some Services Fees*).

Public Interest versus Private Interest

In theory, in a market economy, both private and public interests have the same aim: by pursuing his own private interest an individual, either a consumer or a producer, is contributing to the public good (the invisible hand). The free market mechanism leads to an optimum allocation of resources to the sectors and the companies that are the most profitable (but to whom? to customers, shareholders, the State, the whole economy or all of them). But the market is not perfect. Some private interests do not contribute to the public good and vice versa. The theory of banking regulation [1] is based upon a distinction between public interest and private interest, between a regulation aimed at improving the public good, and a regulation aimed at protecting some private interest (banks', the State's, consumers', depositors', borrowers', etc.). Since the 2008 financial crisis, the notion of public good has been widening to include the stability of the entire economy, including growth, employment, price stability, etc. Unregulated markets are exposed to a monopoly situation, information bias, price distortion and in general all sorts of externalities which interfere in the price structure. In the theory of regulation, rules are not made to build up new constraints, but on the contrary to ensure the free working of a free market.

In the banking sector, risk policy makes a difference between systemic risk and prudential risk, the former affecting the stability of the whole system (public interest), and the latter affecting only an institution (private interest). A risk is said to be "systemic" if the default of one bank impacts the whole banking system and, eventually, the whole economy. The failure of one bank may lead to cash runs and market shrinkage, the long banks being no longer willing to lend to the short banks, which need the cash to square their daily position. The rapidly increasing market rates may entail most or all of the banks withdrawing from the markets and resorting to central bank refinancing. Richard Fuld, Lehman Brother's Chairman, is still convinced that Lehman's failure is owed to the US Treasury, which turned down the request for funds that it willingly extended to Bear Stern bank before Lehman's request, and AIG insurance company right after.

In line with the Chinese tradition of the compassionate mandarin who corrects an inexperienced disciple, the CBRC has a rather "paternalistic" approach to overseeing banks. CBRC directives often interfere in a bank's management. For instance, a CBRC circular listed the qualities and behaviour required from the Board members of banks. If the Board members do not comply with a code of good conduct, they may be dismissed. In a sense, the CBRC as overseer is more demanding than legal requirements.

However, bank regulation may be used for discriminatory purposes: at the expense of foreign banks for instance.

Most bank regulation refers to macro-economic purposes in line with the overall government's economic and financial policy. In 2008 a recovery plan was set up by the government to cope with the financial and global crisis which was threatening China's growth rate. The plan included government subsidies of up to $600 billion. Banks were instructed to increase the volume of credit extended to companies. Within a few months, the volume of fresh loans extended by the banking sector more than doubled (from $800 billion in 2008 to $1600 billion in 2009). However, in some cases, the PBOC and the CBRC's instructions to banks may be much more specific and relate to "private" interests, such as a given loan or a given borrower. In 2016, in view of preventing default from over-indebted companies (most of them State owned companies), 16 banks were requested to swap non-performing loans (or maturing loans) against shares of the defaulting companies.

In China, due to a century-old tradition and government standards, the distinction between public interest and private interest is somewhat blurred. Savers, investors, banks and companies, are all convinced that the government is bound to bail out defaulting banks and companies.

The State as a Shareholder

Government control over the banking and financial sector is managed through the State holding Huijin (Central Huijin Investment Ltd). Huijin's location within the State hierarchy is a sign of the growing importance of the banking and financial system in the government's order of priorities. Originally, banking and financial institutions used to be owned and managed by the central bank (PBOC), while industrial State owned companies were owned and managed by the Ministry of Finance (MOF). Accordingly, Huijin was affiliated to SAFE (State Agency of Foreign Exchange), the central bank's department in charge of managing foreign exchange reserves. This was understandable to the extent that most of the government's ownership of banking and financial institutions used to be funded with foreign exchange reserves. When the sovereign fund CIC (China Investment Co.) was created in 2003, it was first affiliated to the MOF, in charge of the State owned industries. CIC was then cut off from the MOF to be connected straight to the State Council. Then, Huijin was disconnected from the central bank to be transferred to CIC, which acquired the State owned bank holding for $83 billion. However, as a remnant from the past situation, Huijin is a fully-fledged affiliate, with its own Board of Directors and Supervision Board, which has retained a certain degree of autonomy within the CIC organization's schedule. In 2015, in the last step of this game of musical chairs, Huijin Chief Executive, Xia Zhi chun, was set aside, retired and replaced by Xie Ping, while the Minister of Finance, Li Jou wei, was appointed Chairman of the Board.

Huijin has a controlling share in 16 banking and financial institutions: a development bank, CDB (China Development Bank); the four State banks—CIBC (Commercial and Industrial Bank of China), the world's largest bank in terms of assets, CCB (China Construction Bank), the second largest bank in China and one the world's fifth largest in terms of assets, BOC (Bank of China), China's oldest bank, founded in 1912 in charge of international transactions, and ABC (Agricultural Bank of China), China's largest bank network of 35,000 branches; an investment group, Everbright, formed in 1983 in Hong Kong and specializing in banking, stock trading, financial services; insurance (China Life owned 50-50 by Huijin and the MOF) and reinsurance (China Re) companies; security trading companies such as Jiany (China Jianyi Investment Ltd), a trading company turned into an investment bank, Galaxy (China Galaxy Financial Holding Co.), Shenyin & Wanguo (Shenyin & Wanguo Securities Co.), and Guotai (Guotai Junan Securities Co.), a very active trading company used by the PBOC to implement the central bank's operations on the market within the framework of the open market policy. Huijin's asset portfolio is not frozen. In May 2015, Huijin sold $565 billion worth of State financial shareholdings for technical (asset management policy) as well as economic (increase in market capitalization) and political reasons (the policy of widening the role of market mechanisms).

In addition to the banks owned and supervised by Huijin, the State is a direct or indirect shareholder of many companies that in turn hold shareholdings in a number of banks and financial institutions on behalf of the government: SASAC (State Owned Assets Supervision and Administration Co.) which owns State companies; SAFE (State Agency of Foreign Exchange); CIC (China Investment Co.), the government sovereign fund; and NSSF (National Social Security Fund), the government pool of funds that collects and manages the proceeds of social security contributions. Most of the regional banks are wholly or partially owned by local governments.

The Privatization Programme

If nationalizing a private bank or a company is relatively easy, the privatization of a State bank is far more complicated. In spite of a change in ownership, management techniques and government control remain unchanged.

In theory, a market economy is tightly connected to private property and rule of law. In a private property regime, company and household management is the responsibility of consumers and entrepreneurs who are relying on market-led price schedules to make the right decision. Whatever the legal status, Chinese privatizations are not aimed at transferring ownership to private shareholders. Instead, the final aim is to tap public savings, thus diversifying the source of funds, with the view of increasing competition and improving management through market constraints (profit, productivity, innovation). All of the big companies' managers are appointed by or with the consent of the government and are expected to follow government instructions.

When Deng Xiao ping took over power, he was aware that food production was the most pressing issue in a country and an economy which was still mostly agricultural and rural, especially following the dreadful famines of the 1960s that cost 35 million lives. It was a precondition to implement a deep rooted and long lasting economic reform. Within a few months, farmers left the people's communes and switched back to their former lands. The local authorities had to take emergency measures to cope with this new situation and to create *ex nihilo* local institutions: local industries, local banks (credit cooperatives, local government owned banks) to serve the farmers' needs. Local banks were created with the objective of processing payments, collecting deposits and extending loans. However, local banks and credit cooperatives are notoriously ill-managed and do not meet minimum management standards. Loans are granted to well-connected people. Risk management is weak. Credit decisions are biased by local patrons and party secretaries. The geographical basis is too narrow to make possible a sound diversification of risks, resources and assets. Local banks have to be privatized, sold to local investors and/or merged with city banks.

As part of the policy of reform and opening up, old banks were revived: BOC (Bank of China) funded in 1912 to process international transactions; CCB (China Construction Bank), a bank created in 1954 for the financing of infrastructure projects; BOCOM (Bank of Communication), a bank funded in 1908 specializing in the financing of communication projects (railways, telecommunications), a key sector in such a large country that has long been split by foreign powers, local separatism and Chinese warlords; and ABC (Agricultural Bank of China) established in 1951 to finance land reform and the transition to a Soviet type of agriculture. In 1984, ICBC (Industrial & Commercial Bank of China) was funded; it was to become the largest Chinese bank and the largest bank in the world. In 1987 the first State owned commercial bank was established, China Merchant Bank, and 10 years later, in 1997, the first private bank, Minsheng Bank.

The breaking point took place in the early 2000s as part of the Chinese markets' Big Bang. Following the renewal of the ruling team (Hu Jin tao–Wang Jia bao) in 2002–2003, an ambitious privatization programme of all the State banks was implemented, which was intended to boost the development of stock and bond markets. Regional banks followed suit. Regional banks' shareholdings were opened to State companies, foreign banks and sometimes to private groups, but in most cases local governments kept a significant share or at least a minimum share to keep an eye on them. The last step was the creation of internet banks by groups such as Alibaba, Tencent and Baidu (see Chap. 7 on internet banking).

Mainly owing to historical reasons, the wide spectrum of Chinese banking institutions provides a wide range of banking services, scattered all over the Chinese territory, which is well suited to meet the well-diversified needs of local companies.

A Wide Range of Multilayered Banks

The 1985 banking law makes a distinction between different categories of banking institutions: State banks, commercial banks, municipal commercial banks and credit cooperatives. But a comprehensive picture of the banking sector must combine legal and functional definitions (Figs. 4.1 and 4.2).

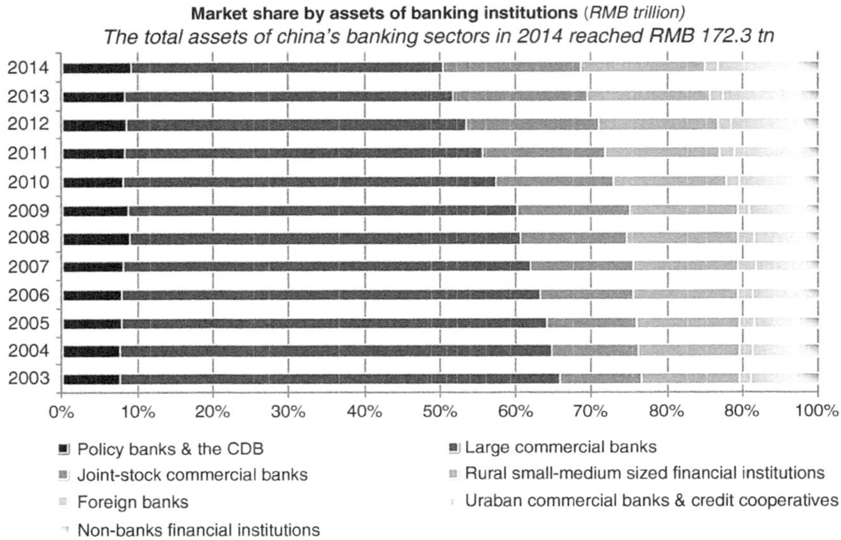

Fig. 4.1 Market share by assets of banking institutions

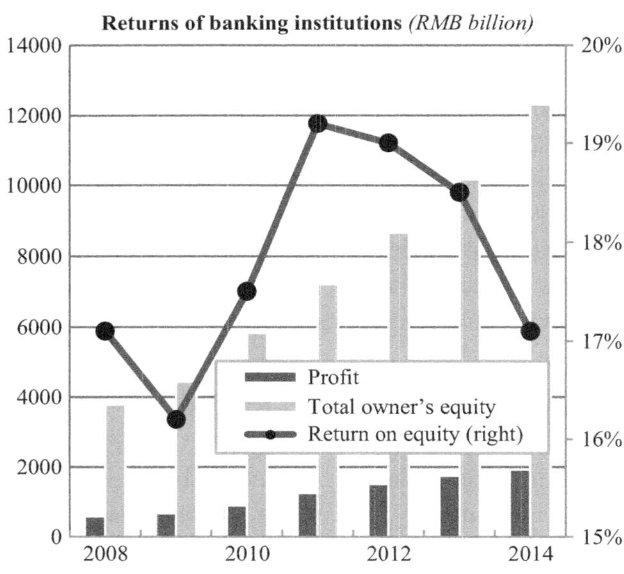

Fig. 4.2 Returns of banking institutions
Source: CRBC

The State Banks

As the suppliers of half the overall credit and two-thirds of bank lending, the State banks have an overwhelming share of China's credit market. The four State banks: ICB (Industrial & Commercial Bank of China), CCB (China Construction Bank), BOC (Bank of China) and ABC (Agricultural Bank of China), are still called "State banks" although they have the legal status of public companies and are listed on the Stock Exchange. The State remains the largest shareholder and whatever their legal statute might be, they are under tight government control. All of the top positions are taken by Party members. The Chairmen are appointed by the Party and the government. The highest officials keep moving from civil service to bank management and vice versa. Zhu Xiao chuan used to be CCB Chairman when he was appointed as Governor of the central bank, the PBOC (People's Bank of China). Shang Fu lin was ABC Chairman when he was appointed as head of the banking supervision agency, CBRC (China Banking Regulatory Commission). In 2012, when the new ruling team was elected, most if not all of the top positions had been removed. Zhu Xiao chuan was not removed, which indicates the greater importance of the role of the central bank and monetary policy. On the other hand, ICBC Chairman Jiang Jian king was not promoted, which was understood to be a sanction.

The present weight of State banks is the result of the privatization process which stretched from 2002 to 2005, following the same pattern: legal change from government institution to public company, increase of capital funds, transfer of bad loans from the banks to four defeasance companies, opening of the shareholding to foreign banks and finally listing the banks on the Stock Exchange. The way that privatization was processed is a sure sign of the way the banking sector is monitored by the government.

In 1984, commercial loans were transferred from the central bank which used to be, from 1952, the only bank fulfilling the functions of both central and commercial bank (processing payments, collecting savings and extending loans) to the newly formed commercial banks. At this time, non-performing loans reached 30% of GDP and 18% of banking assets. In 1999, non-performing loans were transferred to four defeasance companies: Huarong, Cinda, Dongfang and Changfeng.[3] In 10 years the volume of the State banks non-performing loans fell below 1.5% (between 1.2 and 1.3% in 2016) in line with international standards.

In 1998, State banks were massively recapitalized: the government poured $33 billion in capital increase. On the eve of the public offering, a new wave of recapitalization was processed through the State holding Huijin, which in the meantime was removed from the central bank and affiliated to the newly formed sovereign fund, CIC (China Investment Co.). The State Council drew substantial amounts from the rapidly growing foreign exchange reserve allocated to the State banks' capital increases: $45 billion to BOC (Bank of China) and CCB (China Construction Bank) in 2004, $15 billion to ICBC (Industrial & Commercial Bank of China) in 2005, and $10 billion to ABC (Agricultural Bank of China) in 2008. Following the cleaning up of the banks' balance sheets, shareholding was opened to major Chinese and foreign institutions through private placements: Goldman Sachs, Allianz and American Express in ICBC; Bank of America, Temasek (the Singapore sovereign fund), Credit Suisse in CCB; Royal Bank of Scotland, Li Ka Shing (the richest man in Hong Kong and the owner of the Hutchinson Whampoa group), Temasek, Asian Development Bank, Merryl Lynch, UBS in BOC (Bank of China); and Credit Agricole in ABC (Agricultural Bank of China). Finally, HSBC (Hong Kong & Shanghaï Bank), a British bank established in China (in both Hong Kong and Shanghaï) since 1864, took a 19% share in BOCOM's capital.

The State banks reached the final stage of the "privatization" process through initial public offerings (IPOs). The State banks are listed both in Shanghai and in Hong Kong so that foreign banks have access to the issues, either simultaneously (ICBC, ABC) or in two successive transactions (BOC, CCB). The State banks have also sold out a limited share of the equity: 18% of ICBC equity including 6% to Chinese investors (Shanghai) and 12% to foreign investors; 13.6% of CCB's; and 13% of BOC's out of which 2.5% was placed on the Shanghai market and 10% on the Hong Kong market, BOC being the most internationalized of the State banks. The liquidity and the marketability of the State banks'

[3] *Huarong*: Chinese, but also brilliant, magnificent; *Dongfang*: East; *Changfeng*: The Great Wall.

shares listed on the Stock Exchange are limited as two-thirds of the shares are not tradable (A shares). The float (the portion of the shares actually tradable) does not exceed 2% of the ICBC equity, and 0.6% of BOC's, much lower than the standards of foreign stock exchanges. Also the allocation of shares to institutional investors is much higher than the portion allocated to individuals, and the issuing price is at the lowest bracket set by the leading banks, to make sure that the issue is successfully over-subscribed. As a result, the ICBC issue was over-subscribed 75 times for the portion allocated to individual savers, and 12 times for the portion allocated to institutional investors. The BOC issue was over-subscribed 50 times for the portion allocated to individual savers and four times for the portion allocated to institutional investors. When savers who had been queuing the whole night to buy shares from the newly listed company reached the gates of the bank branches, all the shares on sale were already sold out. The bank management had to call the police and the CSRC had to increase the issue by 15%. As the issuing price was much too low, the stock price leaped during the first trading day. The happy few who managed to get some of the newly issued shares made a quick and substantial profit. As the different categories of shares (A, H)[4] are not convertible, a gap was widening between the Hong Kong market price and the Shanghai market price. Later on, as the yuan became more convertible in the aftermath of the 2015 foreign exchange crisis, the gap between the *on-shore* exchange rate and the *off-shore* rate further widened between the two on-shore and off-shore stock prices. From the very first trading day, the BOC A shares (Shanghai) had a 15% discount as compared to the H shares (Hong Kong).

The last one, ABC (Agricultural Bank of China) caused some problems. First, the bank was heavily burdened with bad loans (30% of assets). Second, the government was wondering about its legal structure (a top company holding the local banks or the other way around). The 2008 crisis forced the government to postpone the international listing. Finally, ABC was listed in 2010 through a $20 billion issue on the two markets of Shanghai and Hong Kong.

[4] A shares are listed on the Shanghai Stock Exchange and payable in yuan by Chinese residents, while the H shares are listed on the Hong Kong Stock Exchange opened to foreign investors and payable in foreign currency (US$, HK$ and more recently in off-shore yuan owned by non-residents).

By the end of the privatization programme, the State held a minority participation, out of the 13 Board members six were appointed by Huijin, the remaining positions being allocated to the other Chinese shareholders, the foreign banks and some "independent" members.

The final aim of bank privatization, i.e. the improvement of bank management, proved to be a success. Bank profits rose and the non-performing loans decreased drastically (1.67% on average in 2015). However, the State bank's return is on average half that of the "private" banks' one. They are still overburdened by huge branch networks and a surplus of staff. Due to their quasi monopoly position and government support the State banks are not open to innovation, or to lending to small and medium-sized companies, private companies and high-tech firms.

Political Banks

The political banks—CDB (China Development Bank), CEXIM Bank (China Export Import Bank) and ADB (Agricultural Development Bank)—are called "political" because they are wholly owned by the State and they operate as a strong lever at the government's disposal. The "political" or "development" banks are not allowed to collect the deposit market. Their funding relies entirely on the bond market with a 5-to-10 year maturity and sometimes up to 30 years.

China Development Bank (CBD) is involved in every financing package including international transactions such as acquisitions abroad. CDB is an instrument of China's "Yuan diplomacy" and the "raw material against infrastructures" policy. The role of the development bank is not only to contribute to the financing of the deal, but also to supply some extra financing (soft loans to the local importers of Chinese goods, financing for the construction of infrastructure, linked or not to the supply agreement).

In 2010, CDB extended a $10 billion credit line to Brazil for purchasing made in China equipment and financing infrastructure projects including investing in such critical fields as the petroleum industry. The deal was renewed in 2016. As a result, China became Brazil's largest trade partner in the backyard of the USA. China set up the same type of financing with oil producing Venezuela. In both cases, China appears as a neutral country that does not interfere in local political and economic life and does not care about civil rights. In 2012, China extended a $3 billion line of credit to Greece to be at the disposal of Greek importers, such as shipping companies ordering ships and tankers from Chinese shipyards, as a follow up to the acquisition of the concession of one of the two Piraeus port terminals. In 2015, as part of the recovery plan imposed by the European Union to bail out Greece, the Chinese State owned shipping company COSCO, which is also involved in port management, took over the second terminal concession. Now Piraeus is China's bridge into the European market. During the euro crisis, China bought a substantial amount of sovereign debt, until the members of the euro zone proved unable to come to terms about the then defaulting countries. In 2015, CDB financed the acquisition of the last American chip manufacturer, Micron, by Tsinghua Technology, an affiliated company of the Beijing-based Tsinghua University. In December 2015, CDB extended a seven-year $500 million loan to the Russian company MegaFon, to finance the purchase of electric equipment by Huawei Technology Co. It was the eighth loan in a row granted by CDB to the Russian company.

CDB is also involved in nation-wide domestic investment projects. In February 2015, CDB took a $404 million participation in Tsinghua group, an investment company formed by Tsinghua University with the aim of developing chip manufacturing in China and lowering the Chinese industry's dependence on foreign countries (Taiwan, Korea, Japan).

CEXIM is playing the same role in financing Chinese exports. In this regard, CEXIM was often prosecuted by the WTO (World Trade Organization) for breaching international rules and regulations in export financing. Like the other Western countries, CEXIM is extending soft loans to the exporting Chinese companies, but also to the buyers of Chinese goods. The terms and conditions are notoriously generous (long-term maturities, weak interest rates, deferred interest payments).

In 2014, Montenegro selected two Chinese State companies, China Communication Construction Co. and its affiliate, China Road and Bridge Corp., for the construction of a highway connecting Montenegro and Serbia. CEXIM put together a €687 million ($749 million) 30-year loan.[5] In 2015 a State owned Indonesian coal producer, PT Tambang Batubara Bukit Asam, took a 40% share in a joint venture with China Huadian Corp. to build a thermic (coal) power plant, a field in which China has had lengthy experience. The project was funded up to 75% of the total cost through a $102 billion loan from CEXIM.

Thanks to its centralized decision making process, China is in a position to offer an overall financing scheme provided by a wide range of lending options: shareholding, export finance, project finance, and credit lines for purchasing made in China equipment. In 2015, the cost of two power plants (including one China made 4G) for Argentina was funded through 100% financing. The financing scheme supported Chinese investments and the sale of Chinese equipment in fields such as construction, public works, power plants, etc. Such sectors have a significant weight in Chinese industry and they fit with the long-term policy of keeping control over the sources of raw material much needed by the rapidly growing Chinese manufacturing industry. In 2015 loans to India, Russia and Pakistan in this field increased fourfold. Thanks to its financial and technical expertise, China captured an increasing market share in the fields where it had a comparative advantage. This policy is followed by China's participation in international development banks such as AIIB (Asia Infrastructure Investment Bank), the consortium development bank initiated by China; and NDB (New Development Bank), the BRICS' development bank—all of them competing with the Asian Development Bank and the World Bank (suspected of being under American leadership).

Commercial Banks

In theory, according to the 1985 banking law, there are two types of commercial banks, "public" banks such as China Merchant Bank or Everbright Bank, the banking affiliate of the Everbright financial group, and "private" banks such as Minsheng Bank. In reality, from a purely banking point of view, there is no such difference.

[5] The contract provided that 30% of the workforce should be allocated to the local companies. According to a media enquiry, out of the 4000 workers, there were only 354 Montenegrins.

China Merchant Bank is a State owned bank involved in the government policy of opening up. Based in Shenzen, a special economic zone where Chinese and foreign companies enjoy a special legal and tax status,[6] China Merchant Bank was listed on the Shanghai Stock Exchange (SSE) in 2003, followed by the Hong Kong Stock Exchange (HKSE) in 2006 where 15% of the equity was placed, which priced the bank's value at 2.5 times its book value, a relatively high rate as compared to Western banks. The first issue was oversubscribed 170 times, which would be perceived as a strong mistake in the developed stock markets. The State shareholder could have collected far more money while issuing far fewer shares. However, the State remains the main shareholder through the State owned banks (BOCOM, CCB, BOC) that purchased the new shares. In 2007, Merchant Bank managed to place the full amount of a capital increase amounting to $2.4 billion without losing the controlling interest.

In terms of capitalization, assets and profit records, the "private" bank, Minsheng Bank, is ranked just behind the State banks. The status of "private" bank resulted from close cooperation between private and government interests. Minsheng Bank was funded in 1996 by Jing Shu pin, one of the very few "red" capitalists ("national bourgeoisie" in the Party's terminology) who stayed in mainland China after the 1949 Communist takeover. Minsheng Bank was listed on the Hong Kong Stock Exchange in 2009 and was the first bank from Mainland China to sell its capital to the public. Managed by Eddy T.S. Wang, a former HSBC officer, Minsheng Bank is said to be very well managed. As a consequence, the bank is very active in the Chinese diaspora.[7] Minsheng Bank took a 9.9% participation in United Commercial Bank of San Francisco where an important Chinese community lives. The British bank HSBC formed several joint ventures with Minsheng Bank, including asset management companies, as part of its policy to diversify Chinese banking and financial assets.

[6] To a certain extent the SEZs (Special Economic Zones) have the same sort of status as the nineteenth century "treaty ports" with the main difference being that foreign banks and companies are subject to Chinese law.

[7] Shanghai used to have a strong Jewish community.

Very few "private banks" have been granted a nation-wide banking licence unless they are closely connected with the government. Most of them are relatively small regional banks.

Regional Banks

In the late nineteenth century, when the Chinese Empire was opening up, banks and companies were formed, following the Western model, by the joint initiative of mandarins and merchants; the former providing government support and the latter the financing and management. Today, a number of regional banks are joint ventures and include local governments and entrepreneurs among their shareholders. This is the reason why most of the regional banks are located in the coastal area and in the wealthy east-southern provinces (Fujian, Zeijiang, Guangdong) like the Shanghai-based Pudong Development Bank, the Canton (Guangzhou)-based Guangdong Bank, the Beijing Huaxia Bank, the Fuzhou-based Fujian Industrial Bank, and the Canton-based Bank of Guangzhou.

Tianjin is Beijing's port and provides access from the province of Manchuria to the sea, and an industrial area including the aerospace industry (Airbus, Avic) and related research centres. The Bohai Bank's business area stretches over the provinces of Hebei where Beijing is located as well as the two Manchurian provinces, Jilin and Heilongjian. Among the bank's shareholders are several State companies based in Manchuria such as Teda (chip manufacturer) and Baosteel (iron producer), operating at many sites in Manchuria.

Based in Fuzhou, the capital city of the province of Fujian, the capital of Fujian Bank included local shareholders having local interests: the province of Fujian (25%), Han Sen Bank, an affiliate of HSBC, and IFC (International Finance Company), the banking affiliate of the World Bank when it was listed on the Shanghai Stock Exchange in 1999. The province of Fujian has a long tradition of separatism. In 1949 a number of Fujians followed the nationalist exile to the Taiwan Island, which lies just opposite the shores of the Fujian province. The two sides of the channel maintained strong family, economic, ethnic and linguistic links. Most of Taiwan's investments in China are located in Fujian. In line with the other regional banks, Fujian Bank was listed on the Shanghai Stock Exchange in 2009 to tap public saving and widen its capital base.

Based in Guangzhou (Canton), the capital city of the coastal province Guangdong in the south-east, the Guangdong Bank was created in 1988, relatively early in the reform policy. It belongs to a city and a province viewed as the experimental area for most of the economic reforms. With a network of 500 branches (including several branches in Beijing), $50 billion in assets, 12 million customer accounts, 9 million cardholders and 16,000 company accounts, Guangdong Bank, a regional bank with a nation-wide business area, is a very attractive bank for foreign shareholders (including Citibank).

In 2014, Shang Fu li, head of the CBRC (China Banking Regulatory Commission) made a statement announcing the opening of nine "private" banks on an "experimental" basis in Beijing and Tianjin (Beijing's port city) and in the southern provinces of Zheijian (south of Shanghai) and Guangdong (a coastal province in the far south-east). The opening of "private" banks is tightly controlled by the banking supervision agency. To what extent these banks are "private" is arguable as long as the names of the shareholders are not disclosed.

Urban Commercial Banks

The urban commercial banks are relatively small credit institutions created on the initiative of local government to meet the banking needs of local businesses. Most of the urban commercial banks are still run or managed by local governments. Due to their size and location, urban commercial banks are often ill-managed and exposed to local interference, but they do have a strong local base and customer relationships which make them appealing to foreign investors and banks.

From north to south, the Bank of Dalian is located in a port city (former Port Arthur) in southern Manchuria, an industrial area and research centre through which petroleum and coal production extracted from Manchuria is channelled. The Bank of Qingdao is located in the port city of Qingdao, east of Beijing in the Shangdong peninsula. The Bank of Beijing's business area extends to the Hebei province. Further south is the

Bank of Ningbo, in a port city in the province of Zheijiang, which is connected to Shanghai by a 22-mile bridge, Nanjing Bank located in the city of Nanjing, the former capital city of Chang Kai check's nationalist government (1927–1949), the Bank of Beijing, and the Bank of Hangzhou in the former capital city of the Southern Song dynasty (1127–1279) and a very active industrial area focusing on the pharmaceutical and chemical industry.[8] In the south east, in the very centre of China, the Chongking Commercial Bank, located in the huge city of Chongking (35 million inhabitants), is spreading its business over the upper Yangtsé River.[9]

Rural Credit Cooperatives

With a network of 35,000 credit cooperatives (as many as the ABC's or the Post Bank branch network), the credit cooperatives account for 10% of market share in terms of assets. Most of the credit cooperatives have been formed by local authorities to follow up the policy of reform and opening up initiated in 1978 and to meet the needs of local businesses and households. Today, credit cooperatives are no longer in compliance with modern banking management standards (diversification of the loan portfolio, risk management). Local and central authorities are bringing together rural credit cooperatives to be merged at a later stage with regional banks or city banks.

Post Bank

Following the wave of state bank privatization, China's Post Bank (PSBC) has split its post office and banking business. China's Post Bank is now moving to extend its business range to all of the banking services and to compete on a fair basis with the other Chinese banks. Created in 1919 to offer saving accounts and payment services to households, its business and branch network was extended to the countryside starting in 2007.

---

[8] Hangzhou pharmaceutical industry dates back to the early times of the Chinese Empire.

[9] Bo Xi lai used to be Chongking Party Secretary when he was arrested and charged with "misconduct" (i.e. corruption).

With Rmb 6,800 billion ($1.000 billion) assets, 550 million customer accounts, 40,000 branches all over the country (more than the ABC's branch networks or the four state banks put together), the PSBC (Postal Savings Bank of China) has become a fully-fledged bank. In 2015, the rate of non-performing loans did not exceed 0.87%, far lower than the State banks (1.67%), a rate that raised some suspicions. Once the banking business was transferred to a new entity, the Post Bank privatization process followed the same path as the other State banks. After cleaning its balance sheet, Post Bank capital was opened to domestic and foreign investors and finally opened to the public through an initial public offering. On 28 September 2016 the PSBC raised $8 billion through a listing on the Hong Kong Stock Exchange. Some 17% of the shares on sale were subscribed through a private placement by a group of investors including Alibaba and Tencent, two Chinese internet networks heavily involved in mobile payment, the Swiss bank UBS, and the Singapore sovereign fund Temasek, already involved in a number of Chinese banks, insurance companies and various financial groups.

Credit Guarantee Companies

In 2015, the volume of loans to small and medium-sized enterprises (SMEs) reached Rmb 16,200 billion ($2571 billion), i.e. 30% of the total loan volume, while the SMEs account for 60% of GDP, 50% of tax income and 80% of jobs. In order to expand banking services and credit facilities to SMEs and households, the government imposed quotas on banks and local authorities. However, to meet quota requirements, the banks bypassed the regulation by extending credit to SMEs affiliated to big state companies. Banks are complaining that the SME business is not rewarding enough in view of the risk involved, and that SMEs cannot provide reliable accounting documentation. Finally, the government induced the banks, including foreign banks (HSBC, JP Morgan), and local authorities to create credit guarantee companies aimed at supporting access to credit facilities for small companies, individual companies and farmers.

The State as a Lender of Last Resort

Due to the political and social structure of the Chinese economy, most of the claims end up at government level. The government's primary concern is to prevent bank and company failures, and the subsequent job layoffs that could turn into social disturbances. In the last few years, the number of unprofitable ("zombie") State companies which were kept alive through the extension of bank financing upon government request, has been increasing fast. The number of strikes and social protest has been increasing as well, including those by workers who have not been paid for months, whose social benefits have been cut off, and who have been dismissed in job stricken areas. As a follow up to the new military doctrine which puts the emphasis on technology rather than the mere number of soldiers, the government dispatched a circular to State companies to recruit former soldiers who have been laid off. In a context of growing uncertainty and deteriorating credit risk, banks are subject to shrinking profit margins through the combined effect of an increasing volume of non-performing loans and increasing borrowing costs owing to the liberalization of interest rates. As a result, credit claims are moving up to central government level with the central government becoming a *de facto* lender of last resort.

Increase in Non-Performing Loans

The rise of non-performing loans on bank's balance sheets is due to two cumulative factors: the lending flood in the aftermath of the 2008 crisis and the accounting practices of the State banks. The government's concern was increasing as the actual figures for non-performing loans were in fact hidden by the companies' statutes and the banks' accounting practices (Fig. 4.3).

Following the 2008 global crisis triggered by Lehman Brothers' default in September, and the subsequent recovery plan set up by the Chinese government, banks have doubled the volume of new loans in 2009 as compared to 2008. As a result, a number of bank loans have been allocated to unprofitable investments from State companies, over-capacities,

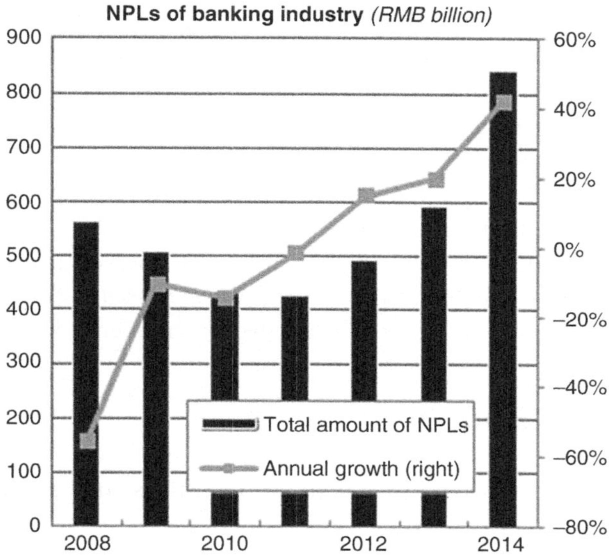

Fig. 4.3 NPLs of banking industry
Source: CBRC

increases in unsold inventory, unused infrastructure from local government, not to mention funds diverted to the purchase of securities which led to the inflated stock market in 2010. The government was forced to send teams of enquirers to investigate the use of government subsidies and bank loans. Later on a number of investment projects were cancelled.

In the following years the government was increasingly concerned by the growing number of state owned companies that were kept afloat through government subsidies, local authority aids and soft bank loans. All of them had an interest in keeping alive the "zombie" companies. The government tried desperately to prevent social disturbances, strikes and layoffs which may hit the Party's legitimacy as the people's shield. The local authorities were concerned about the potential loss of jobs and tax income owing to the closure of the troubled state companies. The State banks were anxious to keep alive huge debtors that could cause substantial losses in the event of default.

The worsening credit situation of State companies takes time to show up in the banks' balance sheets. The loans have to mature until they may be defaulted. From an accounting point of view, the loans are meant to be performing as long as the indebted company pays interest no matter whether or not it is able to redeem the principal. The bank just has to renew enough loans to allow the company to pay the interest, despite the principal, which is covered by implicit state guarantee.

The situation had reached a point where the government had to cope with the State companies' debt and the "zombie" companies. In early 2016, in an effort to remove this critical issue, the government instructed the banks to swap the defaulting loans against company stocks. As a consequence, the banks' rights were weakened in the event of default.

Shrinkage of Bank Profit Margins

Formally, the interest paid by a bank to depositors, and by borrowers to the bank, used to be capped by a government decree issued by the central bank, guaranteeing a fixed profit margin to banks. Officially the capping system is still in force but has been amended by the government. On the deposit side, the rate ceiling is still fixed at 3.3% on one-year bank saving accounts. On the credit side, the floor rate charged to the borrower is set at 4.4%. But the government has authorized banks to issue new investment and saving instruments such as the WMP (Wealth Management Products) and trusts, which provide a much higher return to the subscriber. The new regulation triggered fierce competition between banks to attract new resources. On the other side, the government has steadily loosened regulations governing lending rates. Consequently, banks' profit margins have been shrinking.

The interest rate liberalization was expected to increase competition between banks, which succeeded, and to improve banks' profitability by cutting down costs and increasing the share of service fees in a bank's profit at the expense of interest income that still accounts for 80% of a bank's gross profits (Table 4.1).

The government's action at every stage of the banking business has entailed some biases which distort the market's mechanism and interferes in a bank's management. Most of the banks are directly or indirectly owned by the State and all of them are under tight government control.

Table 4.1 Listed banks' net interest margins (%)

	2008	2009	2010	2011	2012	2013	Q3, 2014
Rising							
China Everbright Bank	2.8	1.95	2.18	2.49	2.54	2.16	2.74
Shanghai Pudong Development Bank	3.05	2.19	2.49	2.6	2.58	2.46	3.04
Industrial Bank	2.92	2.42	2.52	2.52	2.64	2.44	2.77
Bank of Nanjing	3.29	2.80	2.55	2.66	2.49	2.30	2.56
Agricultural Bank of China	3.03	2.28	2.57	2.85	2.81	2.79	2.91
China Minsheng Bank	3.29	2.59	2.94	3.14	2.94	2.49	2.61
China Construction Bank	3.24	2.41	2.40	2.70	2.75	2.74	2.80
Hua Xia Bank	2.07	2.03	2.46	2.81	2.71	2.67	2.71
ICBC	2.95	2.26	2.44	2.61	2.66	2.57	2.60
Bank of China	2.63	2.04	2.07	2.12	2.15	2.24	2.26
Ping An Bank	3.02	2.47	2.49	2.53	2.37	2.31	2.53
Declining							
Bank of Ningbo	3.47	3.12	2.76	3.23	3.48	3.05	2.69
China Merchants Bank	3.42	2.23	2.65	3.06	3.03	2.82	2.50
CITIC	3.33	2.51	2.63	3.00	2.81	2.60	2.37
Bank of Communications	3.01	2.29	2.46	2.59	2.59	2.52	2.40

Source: Company reports

In order to prevent factory closure and bank default, the government is ready to bail out any institution. All the loans in trouble are removed to the bank level. By definition the bank situation is a mirror of the whole economy. In cases of default the government will interfere with the market mechanism to absorb potential losses. Thus, credit claims are climbing up the ladder from company to bank level and from bank level to state level. Every institution, whether creditor or debtor, is relying on a *de facto* State guarantee in case the situation gets worse.

Reference

1. Ping, He Wei. 2014. *Banking Regulation in China*. New York: Palgrave Macmillan.

5

Sidelined Foreign Banks

Within the framework of the policy of reform and opening up initiated in 1978 under Deng Xiao ping's leadership, opening up was as important as reform. Actually, opening up was supposed to be an instrument of reform. From the very beginning of the reform policy, opening the Chinese banking sector to foreign banks was aimed at attracting foreign funds, transferring bank technology and expertise, and stimulating competition in sensitive banking and financial markets.

This is the reason why WTO (World Trade Organization) membership was such a critical issue. Following a tough and lengthy negotiation process, the WTO Membership was finalized in December 2001. In the banking and financial market area, the Treaty provided a five-year grace period granted to China to raise its banks' status to the Western level. By the end of the grace period, China would be committed to opening its banking services market to foreign banks so that they would be treated on an even basis. Until December 2006, foreign banks were prohibited from giving credit in yuan to Chinese companies. They were restricted to making loans in foreign currency to foreign and occasionally Chinese companies. Ten years later, the status of foreign banks is still far away from that of Chinese banks' (Table 5.1).

D. De Rambures, F. Escobar Duenas, *China's Financial System*,
DOI 10.1007/978-3-319-40451-6_5

Table 5.1 Total asset of foreign banks

	2008	2009	2010	2011	2012	2013	2014
Total assets of banking institutions (RMB tn)	63.15	79.51	95.31	113.29	133.61	151.33	172.31
Total asset of foreign banks (RMB tn)	1.34	1.35	1.74	2.15	2.38	2.56	2.79
Foreign banks (% of total)	2.1%	1.7%	1.8%	1.9%	1.8%	1.7%	1.6%

Source: CBRC

In 2016, the foreign bank market share was under 2% of total bank assets. The return on equity (ROE) was half that of Chinese banks (5% against 10%). In 2014, the outstanding bank loans extended by foreign banks represented less than 5% of the total of Chinese companies' indebtedness. In 2015, foreign investors accounted for less than 3% of the total capitalization of the Chinese Stock Exchange. However, regardless of the legal and actual discrimination, foreign banks are still queuing at the CBRC's office to get a banking licence. A foreign bank cannot stay away from a potential market of over a billion people that has been growing at an average rate of 10% over the last 30 years.

A Discriminatory Regulation

By the end of the five-year grace period provided by the WTO Membership Treaty, the CBRC opened the banking market to foreign banks. From 2007 onwards, foreign banks are authorized to open a branch or a 100% affiliate. In addition, foreign banks are authorized to take a 19.9% participation in a Chinese bank or to create a 49% joint venture with a Chinese partner whether it is a bank, a company or a local government. In 10 years the CBRC has granted a banking licence to 176 foreign bank branches.

Foreign affiliates must have a fully paid-up capital of Rmb 300 million ($50 million) and a full branch capital Rmb 100 million ($15 million). If a minimum paid-up capital for an affiliate is understandable, since it is an independent legal entity, it does not seem to be necessary for a full branch that is part of the parent company, the latter being fully responsible for the branch. A joint venture partially owned by a foreign bank is subject to the same legal constraints as a bank fully owned by a foreign bank, even if the foreign shareholder has a minority participation. To get a domestic banking licence, foreign banks must show a profit record over the last three years and a volume of assets over $1 billion. Foreign exchange deposits by Chinese residents cannot exceed 70% of the total foreign deposits by non-residents. A foreign bank branch or affiliate has to keep 30% of its capital funds in convertible foreign currency in a six-month or more current account or savings account, and 30% as Rmb Treasury Bonds or a six-month or more savings account.

A duly authorized foreign bank is not allowed to apply for the opening of a branch unless it has reached $20 billion in assets and recorded profits over the last three years. Every new branch must have minimum capital funds of Rmb 100 million ($15 million). Only a handful of towns are open to foreign banks or branches. The capital funds of a foreign bank branch cannot exceed 60% of the parent company, which proved to be difficult for a foreign bank which has a newly established affiliate with limited capital funds and assets. Foreign banks cannot lend more than 25% of the capital funds to one customer on a consolidated basis.

The legal requirements are softer for foreign banks already established in Hong Kong, which is for foreign banks the most usual way to penetrate the mainland market, and for the Chinese government, a way to strengthen Hong Kong's credit and financial market.

Several banking regulations, which are compulsory to all the banks, domestic and foreign alike, have a greater impact on the alien ones. As part of the policy against money laundering, banks are requested to sign the loan agreement with the borrower himself on the bank premises in order to identify the actual borrower, which is a handicap to foreign banks with a limited number of offices. Banks are requested to lend no more than 75% of the total (non-bank) deposits and the overall lending to one customer (on a consolidated basis) cannot exceed 10% of its capital funds. This is not an impediment to Chinese banks that are big enough to accommodate any customer request, but may be an obstacle to foreign banks with limited capital funds and dealing mostly with big companies, regardless of the capital base of the parent company.

Originally, all of these measures were aimed at setting up some security rules, which is understandable, and to attract foreign funds in foreign currencies, which is no longer needed.

The legal and regulatory requirements are vague enough and undefined so that the market authorities can interpret rules as they wish. The regulation provides that the CBRC must take into account "*the governance, performance, reputation, image of the bank … and the situation of the country where the bank is coming from*". The CBRC can resort to extra requirements, postpone the authorization or withdraw the banking licence at any time and for an unlimited period of time without further explanation. This is the case if a foreign bank no longer fulfils the legal requirements or does not comply any more with CBRC's regulations and directives. Some other measures are aimed at extending Chinese regulation to foreign banks on a par basis. In January 2016, foreign banks were subject to reserve requirements in yuan based upon yuan and foreign currency deposits (then 17.6% of deposits).

In addition to the banking supervisor (CBRC) and the central bank (PBOC), foreign banks have to cope with other national bodies such as the NDRC (National Development and Reform Commission), the SAFE (State Agency of Foreign Exchange), as well as local authorities.

The Withdrawal of Foreign Banks

As part of the privatization programme, foreign banks were allowed to take a stake in the four State banks through private placement ahead of the public offering. Foreign bank shareholding was limited to 19.9% (25% in case of a consortium with Chinese partners). As the offering rate was at the lowest level of the bracket, foreign shareholders made a big profit through added value within a short period of time when the State banks were listed on the Stock Exchange. However, foreign shareholders' participation was frozen by a three to five-year "lock up" provision.

Goldman Sachs took a 4.9% participation ($2.58 billion) in ICBC (Industrial & Commercial Bank of China), further raised to 10% in partnership with American Express and Allianz ($3.78%). Bank of America took a 9% participation in CCB (China Construction Bank) with an option to raise its participation to 19% within five years. RBS (Royal Bank of Scotland) took a 9.6% participation in the Bank of China, later raised to 19%, along with Li Ke chiang, the richest man in Hong Kong and the owner of the Hutchinson Whampoa group, Temasek (a Singapore sovereign fund), Asia Development Bank, Merrill Lynch and UBS. The British bank HSBC (Hong Kong and Shanghai Bank) took a 19.9% participation in BOCOM (Bank of Communications) for $1.75 billion. Credit Agricole took a 19.9% share in ABC (Agricultural Bank of China). Banco de Bilbao took a participation in CITIC (China International Trust and Investment Corp.), the first Chinese investment bank.

Thanks to their costly participation, foreign banks expected to penetrate the Chinese market through the front door, by forming affiliated banks specialized in certain types of credit (consumption loan, real estate credit, credit cards, life insurance, etc). As a reciprocity, foreign banks provided their expertise in sensitive issues like risk management, marketing, innovation, etc. Bank of America created an asset management company in partnership with CCB. Credit Agricole launched an asset management company with ABC (51.3%) and Chinalco (15%), an aluminum group. But the Chinese banks did not feel committed to their foreign shareholders and created affiliated companies with other foreign banks, sometimes competitors of their foreign shareholders. The French insurance group, AXA, managed to create a joint venture with ICBC in spite of Goldman Sachs' shareholding and with Pudong Development Bank in spite of Citibank's shareholders.

However, foreign investors soon realized that regardless of the amount of their shareholding, foreigners had no influence at all on a bank's management. When the financial crisis erupted in September 2008, most foreign banks were instructed to disinvest and focus on their core business. But they were stuck by the lock up clause which prohibited them from selling their shares within a given period of time. In addition, the Chinese authorities were extremely reluctant about the sale of significant shares of State banks' equities at a time when the Chinese stock market was under stress. Foreign banks had to wait until the lock up periods had expired and to sell off their portions step by step over a certain period of time.

In 2009, Goldman Sachs sold half (5%) of its share in ICBC for $7 billion to a group of shareholders including Temasek, Allianz and HSBC which took this opportunity to take a share in the largest Chinese bank and to do the Chinese government a favour which may some day be reciprocated. However, Goldman Sachs is stuck with a frozen and useless participation. In 2009, RBC (Royal Bank of Scotland), which was in serious trouble, sold out its 4.3% participation in CCB capital to a group of Hong Kong investors making a $800 million profit although the CCB share had lost 44% in 2008. UBS sold its share in CCB making a $500 million plus profit. In 2011, Bank of America sold 50% of its participation (5%) in CCB for $8.3 billion, making a $3.3 billion profit. Upon government request, Morgan Stanley was compelled to sell off its 37% share in CCIC (China Capital Investment Bank), China's second largest investment bank, even though the CCIC was initially formed through a joint venture between CCB and Morgan Stanley and has benefited from the involvement, the business experience and the know-how of the American investment bank.

To prevent an impact on the market and a fall in stock prices, the Chinese government resorted to China's institutional investors such as the sovereign fund CIC (China Investment Co.), the foreign exchange fund SAFE (State Agency of Foreign Exchange), the social security fund NSSF (National Social Security Fund) and the State investment bank CITIC (China International Trust and Investment Corp.) to buy back foreign banks' shares as a form of bridge financing. Chinese investment funds—such as CITIC Securities, Harvest Asset Management, Haitong Securities and China Merchant Securities—foreign investment funds—such as KKR, TPG, Blackstone and Carlyle—and sovereign funds—such as Temasek (Singapore), ADA (Abu Dhabi), QIA (Qatar) and SAMA (Saudi Arabia)—took that opportunity to step into the Chinese market. The British bank HSBC bought back the Chinese operations of ING AMRO, the troubled Dutch bank (which was later nationalized), including its stake in Bank of Beijing for $1.5 billion, thus attracting China's benevolence for further transactions.

The New Business Model of Foreign Banks

In response to the 2008 financial crisis, a number of Western banks were requested by the supervisory authorities to withdraw from their peripheral ventures and to concentrate on the heart of their business.

Most foreign banks which took a stake in a large State bank were disappointed by their lack of control over the Chinese bank and their inability to build up joint ventures as a way of gaining entry into the Chinese market. Consequently, most of them moved to a different approach to getting into the Chinese market. This ranged from a "financial" approach, which relied upon the fringe benefit of a sleeping partner, to a large State owned bank, which provided nothing but capital gains and dividends, to a more "industrial" approach in search of synergy, cross fertilization and long-term establishment. In this manner, foreign banks switched from the large State banks to regional banks, especially banks from Beijing and the provincial metropolis (Chongking, Wuhan, Chengdu), the south-east coastal towns (Dalian, Tianjin, Quindao, Fuzhou, Shanghai, Hangzhou, Nanjin, Guangzhou alias Canton) and the coastal provinces (Shantong, Fujian, Jiangsu, Zheijiang and Guangdong) (Table 5.2).

Table 5.2 Foreign and regional banks

Bohai Bank (Tianjin)	TEDA[a], COSCO[b], Baosteel[c]
China Everbright Bank (Hong Kong)	Standard Chartered
Guandong Development Bank (Canton)	Citibank
Pudong Development Bank (Shanghai)	Citibank then BNP
Huaxia Bank (Pékin)	Deutsche Bank[d]
Fujian Development Bank (Fuzhou)	Province of Fujian, Hang Seng
Bank of Guangzhou (Canton)	Scotiabank
Bank of Xian (Xian)	Scotiabank
Bank of Ningbo (Ningbo, Zheijiang)	OCBC (Singapore)
Nanjing Bank (Nankin)	BNP
Bank of Beijing (Pékin)	ING then HSBC
Shenzen Development Bank	Bank of East Asia (HSBC)
Bank of Hangzhou	Commonwealth Bank (Australia)
Bank of Shanghai	HSBC
Qingdao City Commercial Bank	Intesa San Paolo
Chongking Commercial Bank	Carlyle, Dah Sing[e]

[a]TEDA: Integrated circuit manufacturer
[b]COSCO: Shipping company and port manager (such as the Greek Piraeus port)
[c]Baosteel: Largest Chinese steel company and historical partner of Société Générale
[d]Deutsche Bank sold out its stake in Huaxia Bank in January 2016
[e]Dah Sing: Hong Kong-based financial group

From a foreign bank's point of view, participation in regional banks provides a lot of advantages. First of all the investment is less costly while the share in a regional bank can be increased up to 49% as opposed to 19% in a national State bank. In return, foreign banks can expect to have much more influence on the bank's management. In addition their involvement is highly priced by both national and local authorities and the bank's management. Consequently, foreign investment is less vulnerable to changes in government policy or banking regulation. For the national government, the involvement of a foreign bank is a way to improve the bank's management and to stimulate bank competition. For the local authorities, the participation of foreign banks is welcomed as they are hunting for foreign investments, which are a source of jobs and taxes, and a breach in the State banks' monopoly. In addition, foreign banks are expected to extend the business range of a regional bank wholly or partially owned by local government. Finally, the bank's management can expect to gain access to modern banking techniques, to benefit from the transfer of technology and banking innovation. In return the Chinese bank provides foreign shareholders with an existing customer base, a branch network and a clientele of local companies.

To fund their operations, foreign banks can rely upon a customer deposit base and a much lower borrowing cost as compared to refinancing on the interbank market. In addition, regional banks can be listed, issue bonds and undertake capital increases on the stock market. With the proceeds of extra funds raised on the market, banks can enlarge the branch network, invest in new businesses, and maybe get a nationwide banking licence. Thanks to better visibility and a long-term approach, foreign shareholders can invest in employees, funds and techniques.

On top of providing expertise in bank management (risk management, marketing techniques), foreigners have developed a number of joint ventures in areas which were unknown in the Chinese banking business at that time: consumer credit, property loan, real estate, life insurance, credit cards, security trading, asset management, etc. In the wake of the Chinese financial "Big Bang" of the early 2000s, foreign commercial and investment banks had been attracted to the financial market consisting of investment banks, investment funds, stock trading, asset management, etc. Foreign banks had been allocated a larger shareholding (up to 49%), firstly because the investment cost is much lower in the financial services area, but also because foreign expertise was most needed in this field in the earliest development of the financial markets.

The HSBC Case

Created in 1865 in Hong Kong, the Hong Kong and Shanghai Bank (HSBC) is the oldest foreign bank in China, apart from Standard Chartered established in 1854. For a long time HSBC has been deeply involved in the Chinese economy and managed to maintain close relationships with the successive Chinese governments.

Under the Chinese Empire (which collapsed in 1911), HSBC, like all of the other Western banks established on the spot, used to place international bond issues on behalf of the Chinese government on the London market. Following a set of disastrous wars, China had to pay huge indemnities. Western armies were fighting Chinese armies while Western banks sold out China's bond issues on Western markets for substantial fees.

In addition, HSBC financed Western exports of manufacturing goods to China. As Western exporters were unable to sell their products on the Chinese market, they used to resort to local compradores.[1] The Chinese compradores in turn were selling in the deep Chinese market through a network of Chinese merchants (from Shanghai up to the most remote areas of the Yangtze basin: Wuhan, Chengdu, Chongking and beyond). The commodities were purchased through a bank loan extended by Western banks to the compradores against a bank guarantee granted by a limited number of well-known and reliable Chinese family banks (so called Shanxi banks) heading a nationwide network of correspondent banks.

In 1949, HSBC closed its branch in Shanghai and removed its operation back to Hong Kong. Out of Hong Kong, HSBC kept dealing with the new Communist Regime and funding the export of Chinese goods and the sale of Western equipment. In 1993, in anticipation of Hong Kong's return to the mother country, HSBC moved its head office back to London. In 2009, reassured by the new "one country, two systems" policy, HSBC repatriated its operational office back to Hong Kong.

---

[1] From the Portuguese *comprar*: to buy.

HSBC has a very strong market share in China.[2] HSBC assets are split into three different geographical areas: Europe, America and Asia. However, but the Asian area supplies 80% of the profits and half these profits come from the Chinese operations. However, 80% of the profits are made of dividends and capital gains as opposed to 10% only from the branch network.

HSBC has a 19% stake in BOCOM (Bank of Communications) with whom it developed technical assistance (risk management) and a number of joint ventures in various fields of business (consumer credit, credit cards). In addition to the local branches, HSBS owns two banks in Hong Kong, namely Bank of East Asia and Hang Sheng Bank, which have a branch network in mainland China. HSBC also has a branch network in mainland China (110 in 2015), and plans to expand it up to 200. HSBC had a stake in Ping An, the State insurance company, which was sold to the Thai group CP (Chaoren Pokphand) for $9.4 billion making a capital gain of over $3 billion. In answer to the government's request, HSBC created in 2007 the HSBC Rural Bank based in Hubei, a deprived province, to make loans to farmers and small companies.

The Foreign Banks' Market Share

Today Chinese joint ventures are less appealing and a number of foreign banks have disinvested. Now that the Chinese banks and financial institutions have assimilated foreign techniques and know-how, foreign participation is no longer needed. The most prominent Chinese investment banks, such as CITIC and CICC, are now wholly owned by Chinese shareholders. On the other hand, foreign banks are increasingly reluctant to enlarge their commitment to the Chinese market in view of the slowing growth rate and the increasing legal and otherwise discriminatory measures.

[2] HSBC has always been said to be very close to the Chinese government. In 2004 during the students demonstration (the "umbrella" revolution) against the new "election law" imposed by Beijing, HSBC gave a statement saying that the student uprising was "counter-productive". The law provided that only the "patriot" candidates selected by Beijing, would be allowed to compete.

As a result, there is a new wave of foreign bank's disinvestment from the Chinese market. In 2015 Morgan Stanley sold its 19.9% stake in Hangzhou Industrial & Commercial Trust which it acquired in 2008. Macquarie, the Australian financial group heavily involved in infrastructure, sold its 19.9% interest in Sino-Australian International Trust which it acquired in 2009. Barclays, the British bank, reduced its stake in its Chinese joint venture, New China Trust, from 19.5% to 6%. Deutsche Bank, which is under pressure in its home market, sold out its stake in Hua Xia Bank to PICC Property and Casualty Cy., a State owned insurance company for somewhere between Rmb 23 billion and Rmb 25.7 billion ($3.6 billion and 3.9 billion). There are only 17 foreign banking ventures left in China (as of 2016).

The government policy regarding foreign banks is now well defined. Foreign banks are welcomed as long as they are contributing to the improvement of the Chinese banks' management, the import of banking and financial innovation, and the stimulation of market competition. However, based upon restrictive regulation and discriminatory measures, foreign banks are purposely kept in a marginal position. None of them is in a situation to seriously compete on an even basis with Chinese banks and financial institutions. The business arena of foreign banks' branches and wholly owned affiliated banks is quite limited. In addition, foreign banks are under the threat of a change in government policy and may be forced to give up the investments they have built up over years. Nonetheless, foreign banks are still applying to penetrate the Chinese market in one form or another or to enlarge their local operations. Whatever the returns from their Chinese business, foreign banks cannot ignore such a large and fast-growing market.

6

Credit Black Market

According to a central bank annual report (2015), non-bank lending accounts for 30% of the total bank credit in China. In the same report, there is a discrepancy between the growth of money supply and the growth of credit supply. Given that money creation is owed primarily to bank credit, there is a leak in the money supply. A number of companies and households that have no access to bank credit turn to the informal credit market. In this regard, the fast growth of non-bank lending is a sign of a financial system that is unsuitable for the needs of the economy. However, informal credit is not specific to China. In the UK, non-banking credit accounts for 3.5 times GDP and 8 times the volume of banking credit [1]. In China the high level of non-bank credit is both a sign of a highly sophisticated alternative source of lending and a remnant of old lending practices.

D. De Rambures, F. Escobar Duenas, *China's Financial System*,
DOI 10.1007/978-3-319-40451-6_6

In the IMF's Financial Stability Report (2015), non-bank credit includes the financial assets of monetary funds, investment funds (hedge funds, trust companies, private equity funds) and non-banking financial companies involved in lending. A great number of financial institutions are investing excess funds in monetary funds, while waiting for the right investment, with the goal of improving the return of the overall portfolio. In its report, the IMF is increasingly concerned about the growing number of non-bank credit instruments: inter-company loans (B2B or business-to-business), online lending platforms, sub-prime types of credit, etc. so that loans are removed from the banks' assets. In so doing the banks gain more room for further lending within the regulatory limits of the banks' balance sheets (Table 6.1).

The growth of non-bank credit is a worldwide phenomenon. Over a 10 year period, the volume of non-bank credit has trebled, from $25 billion in 2002 to $75.5 trillion in 2013, i.e. half of the increase in bank loans and a quarter of the financial assets. The volume of non-bank credit in relation to bank credit is uneven from one country to another. It amounts to 179% in the USA where company financing is split 50-50 between bank loans and non-bank credit, 60% in the euro zone where companies prefer to finance themselves via bank credit rather than via financial markets and 55% in emerging countries (30% in China). The risk involved in non-bank credit is said to be "systemic" by the IMF as this type of credit is not subject to banking regulation.

Table 6.1 Shadow banking

Assets (% *GDP*)		
Country	Shadow banking	Bank credit
Canada	92.1	217.6
UK	354.4	800.5
Germany	72.4	274.2
Russia	3.5	84.4
China	25.8	257.3
Japan	52.0	343.9
USA	165.9	95.6
France	96.2	366.0

Source: *Financial Times*, 2014

Based on the above statistics, the volume of informal credit in China is relatively low compared to other countries such as the USA and the UK. In 2014, China's non-banking credit amounted to 4% of the total non-banking credit for an economy which accounts for 21% of world GDP. Non-banking credit in China is growing fast despite being relatively unknown. By definition, the volume of informal credit is hard to quantify. The volume of loans provided by the shadow, unregistered, local credit companies is also unknown. In addition, crowdfunding is growing fast but the average lifetime of such companies is so short that a number of transactions do not come to light. As most credits are short term or even very short term, turnover is much higher. In 2013, registered non-banking credit reached 10% of outstanding loans (25.6% of GDP against 257.3% of bank credit) while they accounted for 43% of the loans falling due (Figs. 6.1 and 6.2).

In China, State banks are dealing primarily with State companies and local governments which enjoy a *de facto* State guarantee. They are reluctant to lend to private companies, small and medium-sized companies and high-tech companies, on the grounds that they are not able to provide reliable accounting documentation and by definition have no or very little collateral to back up the loans.

Informal credit is an obstacle to an efficient monetary policy. In accordance with government practice, informal credit is neither authorized nor forbidden; it is tolerated. Informal credit may be harmful to the implementation of monetary policy and financial stability, but it is necessary. It lies in a grey area which fluctuates according to credit availability. In the event of credit shrinkage, companies and households turn to the informal market. This is especially noticeable in the property loan market. When the central bank took steps to slow down the volume of property loans in order to prevent a swelling bubble, most households, and property and real estate companies, went to the alternative informal credit market. The growth of informal credit has both structural factors (an unsuited banking system) and short-term factors (credit shrinkage). Some industries are more vulnerable to credit shortage: property and real estate, exporting industries, food industries, farms and rural firms, family businesses and internal provinces.

The legal nature of lending companies ranges from registered companies to unofficial pawnbrokers.

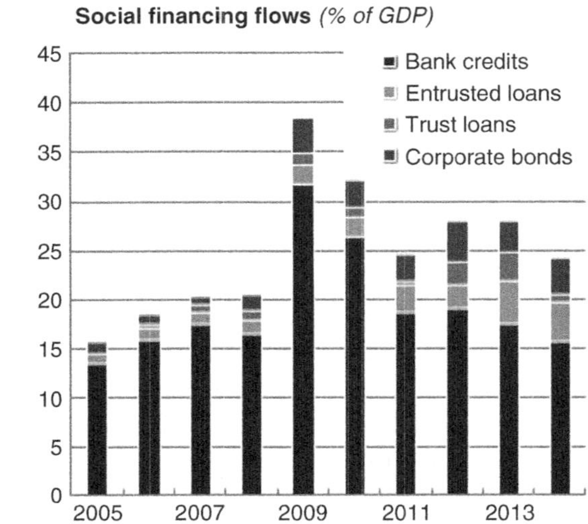

Fig. 6.1 Social financial flow
Source: OCDE

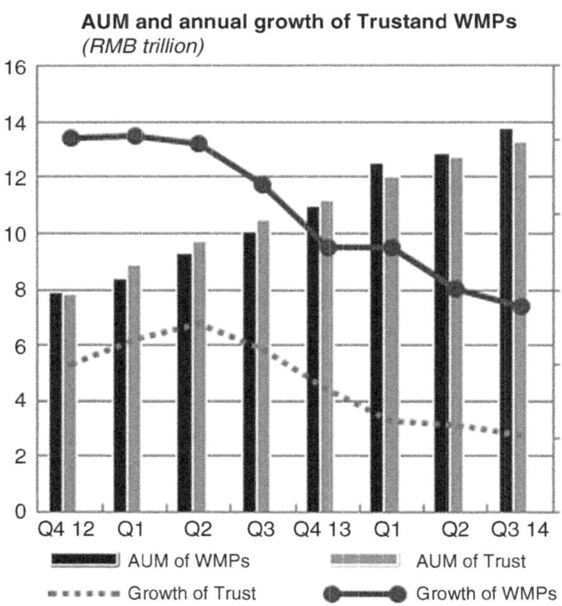

Fig. 6.2 AUM and annual growth of trust and WMPs
Source: CBRC

Traditional Forms of Credit

For centuries local lenders have responded to the borrowing needs of their neighbours:[1] for example, to finance a farmer whose crop is not yet ripe and sold. The loans were granted on a short-term, sometimes very short-term, basis (a few weeks or even days). In some cases, the interest rate was computed on a daily basis. The loan could be aimed at business financing: relatives, friends, neighbours got together to finance a new venture. It could also be for what falls within a consumer type of credit: the studies of a child, a family event such as weddings or funerals that are a matter of prestige as well as filial devotion, or the purchase of a house, a bank loan reimbursement, a child going abroad to study or in search of a better job … The *dahui* (encounter loans) are subject to unwritten rules but the default rate is much lower than with bank credit as the family's reputation is at stake. Social pressure is much more compelling than a written contract and no claim has ever been brought to court.

A *Tsing Houei*[2] agreement is a sort of mutual credit. Several lenders get together to extend a loan or to finance a business project (the purchase of a shop or the funding of a new restaurant). Once a year the partners get together for lunch at the borrower's expense and draw lots: the winner has the option either to withdraw his share or to reinvest the proceeds in the loan. Every year one partner exits and one partner enters.

However, the lending company may be a large one listed on the Stock Exchange. Credit China, an informal credit business based in Shanghai, grants loans within one or two weeks (as opposed to one or two months for ordinary banks) at very stringent conditions regarding the interest

[1] Mao Tse toung's father, Mao Yi chang, was a local "notable" from Shaonan (Hunan province) who built his wealth from pawnbroking.

[2] "*Houei*" means "put together", "partnership".

rate, maturity and collateral. Credit China, a non-bank private lending company, was listed on the Shanghai Stock Exchange in 2010 followed by several bond issues. On this occasion a State company, Shanghai Xinhua Publishing Group Ltd., took a Rmb 1 billion stake ($150 million) in Credit China capital. In 2014, Credit China had Rmb 74 million ($11.7 million) of past due loans, i.e. 9.1% of the total outstanding loans. In 2010, a Shanghai-based real estate company, Yuhu Investment Co., built an office building in the Songjiang area, an industrial area of Shanghai. One year later, the building was still empty and Yuhu was considering converting the building into a retirement home. In 2011, Yuhu Investment borrowed Rmb 60 million ($9.5 million) from China Credit backed by a mortgage on the building. Unable to meet the repayment schedule, Yuhu Investment was forced to sell a shopping centre in the middle of the city of Shanhai to China Credit at a price much lower than the market price.

Some lenders are trading under the cover of micro-finance institutions. When the above transaction was made public, China Credit's shares quoted on the Shanghai Stock Exchange lost 57% within a year. Mr Ting, China Credit's owner, moved to Chongking where he lauched a micro-credit company.

However, this type of credit is very risky. Lending companies are funded through the sales of shares or the opening of saving accounts, and through bank credit. Depositors are granted a much higher rate of return than the market rate. But the unregulated lending companies are very weak. In January 201, Hanquio, an investment company (a "trust" legally) from the Jiangsu province (a coastal province north of Shanghai), closed its doors without notice. In 2014, an investment company, Shanxi Platinum Assemblage Investment, in the Shanxi province, offered a 14–18% return to depositors. Unable to meet the bank loan repayment schedule, the company defaulted and the owner suddenly disappeared.

However, in view of the number of small denomination loans scattered all over the Chinese economy, informal credit may have a systemic effect on an area or an industry. In the port city of Wangzhou in the Fujian province (near Taiwan) a number of exporting firms specializing in mass consumption products (textile, shoes, toys) are based. Following the bankruptcy of one of the lending companies, the whole industry in this region and all of the banks were hit by a domino effect and went bankrupt.

As the crisis was made public in the domestic and international media, the government had to intervene. As a follow up, the government initiated an experiment in the Wangzhou area, with the aim of inducing lending companies to show up as legally registered and regulated entities. However, the government is in a difficult situation when it comes to unofficial lending companies because a large portion of Chinese companies and households depend on informal credit firms.

Bank Disintermediation

Bank credit accounts for 80% of total business financing; the rest is equally shared by financial markets and informal credit. Only the largest firms, most of them State owned, have access to financial markets. Small and medium-sized companies that are neither big enough to have access to bank credit nor have sufficient fixed assets as collateral for a bank loan and have exhausted their borrowing capacity or are no longer liable for bank credit, turn to informal credit.

In fact, informal credit is suited to all parties involved: to borrowers, it is an alternative and often the only source of funds; to lenders it is a way to make huge profits through interest collected and the sale of collateral; to savers and depositors it is a very profitable investment opportunity; to banks that are lending to informal credit companies it is not only a profitable investment, but a way to write off loans from their balance sheets and to rebuild their lending capacity. And finally, for the government it is a source of credit available to a number of small and medium-sized companies that play a critical role in job creation, provide tax income, productive investments and exports, and increase competition in the banking industry.

Trust

"Trusts" are investment companies that purchase loans from banks. Trust companies are funded through the sale of shares and bonds on the market, and the opening of saving accounts in their books. Trust companies often turn to bank credit to refinance the acquisition of loans. However, in spite of (or because of) the high rate of return, the investment in a trust company is a risky venture as depositors do not know the final borrowers included in the loan portfolio. On the other hand, a number of banks resort to "trust" companies to write off sensitive loans. Sometimes the trust company is created upon the initiative of the bank itself, with the aim of selling off sensitive credit.

In 2014, CCB (China Construction Bank) had a Rmb 45 billion ($750 million) lending position on Lisheng Group, a steel company that turned out to be unable to repay the loan, like many other Chinese steel companies. Within the framework of a debt restructuring scheme, CCB sold out part of the claim to three local, unidentified, Shanxi "trust" companies. In return, the trust companies took a Rmb 3 billion ($450 million) capital share in Linsheng Group, while CCB agreed to make an extra loan up to Rmb 2 billion ($300 million) against a 50% capital share of Linsheng. It turned out that the local government was one of Lisheng's shareholders. In any case, the local authorities were concerned and wanted to keep the company alive to prevent further layoffs and potential workers' strikes. As a result of the restructuring scheme, Lisheng's credit risk was transferred from a bank to an investment company and ultimately to the savers who subscribed to the shares of the investment company. However, the ultimate depositors had no recourse against the bank in case of default.

In 2014, the State bank, ICBC (Industrial & Commercial Bank of China), had a Rmb 3 billion ($496 million) credit position on Zengfu Energy Group, an unknown Shanxi mining company owned by a former farmer turned businessman (now behind bars). As with many other mining firms, Zengfu was on the verge of bankruptcy. On top of that, the government had undertaken measures to wind up the near bankrupted mining companies and to close the pits that did not meet minimum safety standards. In anticipation of the coming bankruptcy, ICBC created an *ad hoc* "trust" fund called "Credit Gold Equals No 1" to which ICBC sold the loans of the ailing company. ICBC sold the shares of the trust fund to 700 of its customers. In return, the Credit Gold fund sold the loan to a fund called CCT (China Credit Trust). CCT was controlled up to 30% by the State owned insurance company PICC (People's Insurance Company of China Ltd.). After purchasing the loan to Zengfu Energy Group, CCT had converted the credit into a three-year loan. At maturity, Zengfu was not in a situation to meet its obligation and pay back the loan. CCT informed the shareholders that they would not be reimbursed. ICBC turned down the shareholders' request for reimbursement, stating that the bank had no commitments.

Trust funds are tightly linked to the banking sector that has refinanced most of the loans transferred to the new lending units. In this context, the trust fund business is highly "systematic" by nature.

P2P Credit

P2P (Peer-to-Peer or Person-to-Person) credit is nothing but an old lending practice renewed through the use of modern technology: a website is a way to broaden the scope of lenders and borrowers far beyond the circle of friends and relatives. As a widely enlarged communication tool, a lending platform groups the financial services—creditworthiness of the borrower, legal documentation, cash collection, fund depository—but in principle the platform is nothing more than a credit agent that does not act as a lender.

In 2015 there were more than 2000 online credit platforms free of any regulation, and beyond the central bank's supervision. The volume of P2P credit has escalated over the last few years, from Rmb 22.8 billion ($3.7 billion) in 2012 to Rmb 103.6 billion ($16.8 billion) in 2014,[3] which ranks China ahead of the USA. Although websites are acting as agents and not as principals, the lifetime of the lending platforms is quite short. Every year, the number of sites closing equals the number of brand new ones. The loans are usually short-term loans at a very high interest rate, but they are highly dangerous as depositors know virtually nothing about the borrowing companies or individuals.

Based in Beijing, Diarong.com, is a P2P e-lending platform created in 2012 by two partners, Soul Hittite, a former manager of Lending Club, and Kevin Guo, a lawyer specializing in property law. They managed

[3] Wangdaizhijia, the largest P2P credit site.

to raise funds from several investors, including a private equity fund affiliated to Standard Chartered and two American funds, Tiger Global and Global Management. According to Diarong's management, the average customer is, for example, an Uber taxi driver who needs a loan to buy a car using the collateral of a leasing company.

B2B Intercompany Credit

During the times of the Planned Economy (up to 1992), company managers had to wait for instructions from many official bureaucratic institutions: the Plan administration, the Ministry of the relevant industry, the Ministry of Finance, the central bank, etc. to get permission to pay, and to wait for the delivery of funds needed to order equipment, material and sub-products (or more often to settle workers' pay). As a consequence, most of them managed to get in touch directly with the supplier's company for an off-the-record transaction.

Today, some of the old practice remains. Even though it is prohibited by law, some companies are resorting to other companies' lending. For the borrowing company that has exhausted its borrowing capacity, this is an alternative source of borrowing. To the lending company, it is an opportunity to get a better return on its cash liquidities. To the bank, it is a way to lower its credit exposure and increase its lending capacity. The bank is nothing but an agent, but in some cases it provides its guarantee to facilitate the transaction. In such cases, the transaction should be recorded in the off-balance sheet account.

In 2014, a Nankin-based shipyard, Sainty Marine, offered a Rmb 90 million ($14 million) one-year credit deal at an 18% interest rate to Nanjing Fudi Property Developing, a real estate developer. At maturity, the borrower was not able to reimburse the loan. Sainty Marine referred the matter to the Court. In accordance with the law, the Court should have condemned the company for illegal lending practices. Instead, the Court condemned Nanking city (as one of the developer's shareholders) and seized Nanjing Fudi's assets to reimburse Sainty Marine. The magnitude of the loan was very small compared to overall company debt ($15 million out of $400 million).

In some cases, a company loan is converted into a bank loan, so that the credit figure is wiped off the lending bank's assets and is no longer computed with the credit quotas and ratios. The loan is transferred to another bank's balance sheet while the lending bank makes a deposit of the same amount in the new bank (with or without a bank guarantee). Otherwise, the lending company may lengthen the terms of payment granted to a supplier, a form of disguised credit facility.

Banking Acceptances

Another way to bypass banking regulation is the issuance of bank acceptances. An increasing number of Chinese companies are getting paid through bank acceptances. In case of credit shrinkage or when banks have reached their credit ceiling, they turn to bank acceptances to keep processing their customers' payments. In exchange, bank's customers can use the bank acceptances to settle their own payments. From then on, through such endorsement (like the discounting of a letter of credit), bank acceptances can move from hand to hand.

In the 2013 interbank market crisis, banks were increasingly reluctant to lend to each other, for fear of getting stuck in a bank default. To keep the payment process working and to provide some liquidity to the interbank market, the PBOC allowed banks to issue bank acceptances to settle their customer payments. Even if the payment was not finalized in the case of a company's default, bank acceptances kept circulating as a fully-fledged currency. In 2014, the central bank instructed banks to repatriate the entrusted loans (without bank guarantee) and the trusted loans (with bank guarantee) into the bank's balance sheets.

Local Government's Borrowing Vehicles

In the early years of the reform policy, a certain number of duties had been transferred to local governments, within the framework of the decentralization policy. As a consequence, local authorities undertook lavish spending on useless infrastructures unable to produce enough cash flow to meet the repayment schedule. The expenditure spree of local authorities led to swelling inflation which caused the 1989 Tien An Men uprising. For several years, the inflation rate went unchecked. Jiang Ze min, then Party Secretary and Chairman of the Republic, appointed Zhu Rong ji, a former governor of the central bank, as Prime Minister (1998–2003). An energetic and experienced official, Zhu Rong ji managed to repatriate the tax policy (both tax income and expenditure) back to the central government. From then on, fiscal policy was under tight government control.

Since then, local authorities are prohibited from borrowing without the central government's permission. But local authorities are squeezed between increasing liabilities and decreasing tax income. They have to resort to illegal taxes or borrowing to square the local budget. In order to finance off-budget expenditure, local authorities are borrowing through LGFVs (Local Government Financing Vehicles) to get the most needed additional resources. Most of borrowing costs were covered through sale of land owned by the local government or seized from farmers (purchased at a very low price). In addition, some local officials, such as the province governors, are far too powerful within the Party hierarchy to be reined back under the central bank's control.

In 2013, according to the government audit office, the overall indebtedness of local government amounted to Rmb 17.9 trillion (the last available figure), not including hidden debt through ad hoc borrowing vehicles which have been growing fast over the last few years as local government spending increased faster than incomes. Local government debt accounted for one-third of total bank credit and one-fifth of GDP. The central government removed additional expenditure to local governments without the subsequent income. In 2015, according to government sources (*China Securities Journal*) the outstanding LGFV debt amounted to Rmb 7660 billion ($1215 billion), out of which 26% (Rmb 2 trillion or $350 billion) was risky. The repayment of only 24% of local government debt was budgeted for. The land resources allocated to local debt repayment were drying up. For the first time, the amount of land used for new property development in China fell more than 25% in 2014.

In 2015, the overall outstanding debt of local governments was estimated to be up to Rmb 154 trillion ($2.5 trillion) in 2013, i.e. a third of total bank credit and 20% of GDP. In May 2015, the government

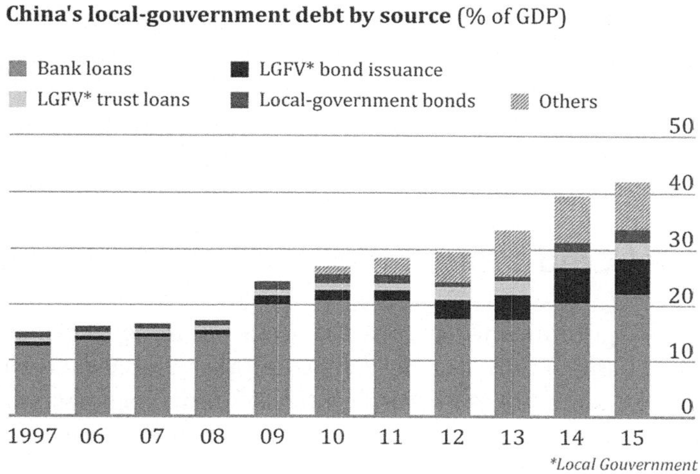

Fig. 6.3 China's local government debt by source
Source: IMF, Bank for International Settlements

stated that the volume of problematic loans owed by local governments amounted to Rmb 22 trillion ($3.5 trillion). According to some sources, the overall debt of local administrations may reach as much as $10 trillion in the coming years, which is in line with the above figure (Fig. 6.3).

The central government tried to get local government borrowing under control. In October 2014, it restated that local governments were not permitted to borrow through so-called LGFVs. However, the government authorized local governments to borrow on a case by case basis. In May 2015, the government issued a plan to refinance $1 trillion loans maturing in the same year. In June 2015, the government permitted provinces to issue Rmb 2.6 trillion ($419 billion) in bonds in view of securitizing the outstanding bank loans owed by local authorities. The proceeds of the loans were expected to be used to swap short-term bank credit against long-term bonds. But the market remained skeptical. In April 2015, the Jiangsu province was forced to postpone a Rmb 64.8 billion ($10 billion) bond issue due to lukewarm demand. However, in May 2015, Jiangsu sold 10-year bonds at a yield of 3.41%, slightly above the government's bond rate of the same maturity, 3.37%. Finally, in early 2016 the government backpedalled. Banks were instructed to swap bank loans against company shares.

Whatever the debt situation of local governments is, central government's concern is obvious. The central government is said to be thinking about the creation of a centralized government agency to borrow on behalf of local governments. This would be the first step towards developing a market similar to that of the US municipals.

Informal Credit Regulation

The Chinese government has mixed feelings regarding informal credit. On the one hand, informal credit is a credit leak, a source of credit which is beyond the central bank's control. Informal credit is an obstacle to the effectiveness of monetary and credit policy. Because of the connection of informal credit with the banking sector (a number of informal credit entities are funded through bank loans), with stock exchanges (a number of informal credit companies are listed on the Stock Exchange), and in general with the many companies borrowing through the informal credit market, the growing weight of informal credit in the Chinese economy at large is a potential source of "systemic" risk in the case of bankruptcy, spreading all over the banking and financial markets and beyond. Also, informal credit is a sort of black market that channels funds from corruption and money laundering. On the other hand, the government must take into account the many companies (small and medium-sized companies, private companies, high-tech companies, etc.), that play a critical role in the Chinese economy but that have no access to bank credit. To these companies, the informal credit market is the only source of funds.

In 2015, the State Council created a working group, including all parties involved, to set up the framework to regulate the informal credit market. The issue is being handled by a number of competing and overlapping government bodies: the central bank (PBOC), CBRC (China Banking Regulatory Commission) which supervises the banking sector, CSRC (China Security Regulatory Commission) which supervises the stocks markets, CIRC (China Insurance Regulatory Commission) which supervises the insurance market, and many other State entities. In addition, a "task force" was set up to look into and prosecute illegal, informal, credit companies. According to the government press agency, Xinghua, 75 P2P platforms went bankrupt and 72 websites were closed in 2013. Given that informal credit plays such an important role in the Chinese economy, it is questionable that a mere task force enquiry could be enough to keep control over such a huge grey area.

Reference

1. Shadow and Substance. 2014. Special Report. *The Economist*, May 10.

7

Fast Growing Internet Banking and Finance

In 2015, upon instruction from the State Council, the China Banking Regulatory Commission (CBRC), the banking supervision agency, granted six banking licences to non-banking institutions "on an experimental basis". This initiative was aimed at spurring competition in the banking sector, promoting financial innovation and diversifying the range of banking products and services. With 600 million internet users who are already processing 50% of their shopping through online sale sites (against 20% in France and 33% in the UK), and 40% of global users of mobile banking through smartphones, China is already the world's largest market. According to the World Bank, 55% of Asians, 64% of Chinese and 90% of Americans have a bank account. China has great growth potential.

In 2015, the government launched an ambitious "digitalization" programme focusing on mobile internet, data cloud storage and Big Data technologies. To follow up, a number of Chinese cities have developed "scientific parks" such as the Beijing-based Zhongguancun created in 2012, to get together entrepreneurs, universities, start-ups, business angels, high-tech enterprises and research centres. While the rural migration to cities and the one child policy broke down traditional social

D. De Rambures, F. Escobar Duenas, *China's Financial System*,
DOI 10.1007/978-3-319-40451-6_7

relations (family, neighbours, friends, relatives), internet banking is recreating "virtual communities" much larger and much wider than the usual banking network [1]. Internet networking allows banks to reach the most remote areas and social layers that have no access to banking services. The banking network, over-burdened by bureaucratic expenditure, over-staffed, and protected by a monopoly situation and favourable banking regulation, is unable to follow the transition. The government bypasses this obstacle by granting banking licences to non-banking institutions. The development of e-banking supported by the authorities is a good example of the way the government is using market mechanisms to enforce banking competition and stimulate financial innovation.

In banking and financial markets, innovation does not generate new types of products but new types of marketing: "The message is no longer the content, but the media" [2]. The development of e-banking puts together a banking unit combined with an internet network. However, online banking is not only a new marketing technique, but also a new business model. It is understandable that the existing networks, which have collected a huge amount of customer data, must be properly equipped to jump into the banking and financial markets. In e-banking business, the market is much larger, and information costs as well as operating costs are much less. As a consequence, the interest rate paid to depositors is higher and the interest rate charged to borrowers is lower; the minimum level of transaction is much lower, as are the new entrants' fees. By lowering borrowing costs, online banking is particularly well-suited to micro-finance, consumer credit and financial services. In this regard, credit platforms and e-banking are beneficial to the economy as a whole and more generally to the entire community. Through online banking, Chinese savers gain higher rewards from different types of investment offers. As a comparison, the return from a bank savings account is 3%, from a short-term Treasury bond 3.4%, from a WMP (Wealth Management Product) marketed by the bank 4–6%, and from short-term credit extended through a lending platform up to 10%.

Taking advantage of the wide network of users, the customer database provides useful information about a customer's purchasing and investing behaviours. Now interest is moving to non-banking, non-internet companies, such as Wanda (real estate, tourism, hotel, entertainment and the film industry), Macrolink Real Estate (property) and Suning Commerce (direct sales) have already applied for banking licences.

Saving Instrument Marketing

In 2014, 44% of investment funds had been marketed through internet networks. They were offering a much higher return than saving accounts or other banking products combined with a higher liquidity. A number of investors have disinvested, removing their savings from bank funds to funds marketed through internet networks. The monetary funds sold through Alibaba are available without notice at any time. On the State's CCTV television network, Alibaba was said to be "a vampire sucking the banks' blood".

In a first step, the largest networks like Alibaba, Tencent and Baidu marketed investment funds managed by banks or investment companies. In a second step, internet networks created and marketed their own funds. Alibaba's fund, Yu'e Bao,[1] launched in 2013, was distributed by Ant Financial through the group's payment arm, Alipay, an affiliated company of Alibaba. In two years Yu'e Bao had collected Rmb 578 billion ($98 billion), which is already the largest Chinese fund.[2] Climbing up the value chain, in 2006 Alibaba acquired THAM (Tian Hong Asset Management), an asset management company. Thanks to the customer data collected by Alibaba's network of e-commerce, the group is in a situation where it can optimize its marketing policy.

Payment Service

In a first step, Alibaba created a payment affiliate, Alipay, to process payments related to the e-commerce platform. Alipay's customers can keep the excess cash on their current accounts opened between transactions. The customers' accounts are paid an interest amount, like bank savings

[1] *Bao*: "Treasury" in Chinese.

[2] Z-Ben Advisors, 2004–2016, http://z-ben.com/.

accounts, or customers can use the proceeds to subscribe to an investment fund. The Alibaba service payment offers a better return without going to the bank office next door. As opposed to banks, Alipay does not need a banking licence and is not subject to the same legal constraints as ordinary banks. As a final step, Alibaba has applied to get a banking licence (Fig. 7.1).

Alipay (Alibaba) and Wepay (WeChat, Tencent) are already the leading online banks with a market share of respectively 79.5% and 12.9% of new deposits, followed by Lakala.com, Yeeplay and Baidu Money. Of the 700 million internet users, 360 million have already used a mobile payment. In 2015, total e-payments experienced a 57% increase to Rmb 9000 billion ($1400 billion). A customer can make a payment by scanning the shop keeper's QRcode. While Alibaba has an overwhelming market share in computer e-payment, Tencent managed to hold a leading position in mobile banking, thanks to its leading position in the smartphone market. As online shopping is slowing down because of increasing competition and a growing number of competitors in the market, e-commerce sites

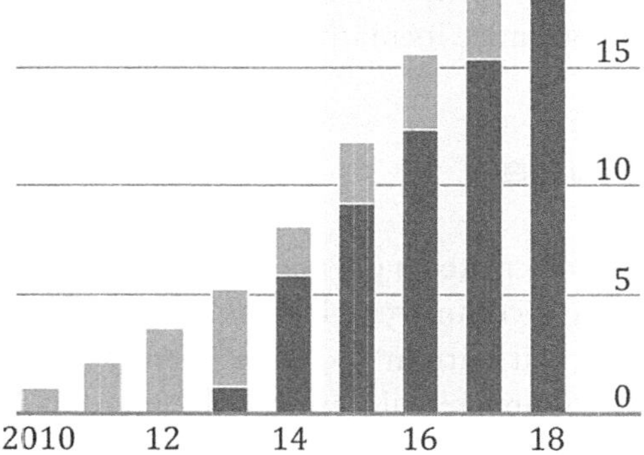

Fig. 7.1 China online and mobile payments
Source: IResearch report, 2015–2018 forecast

are now identified as a new source of growth through the development of on-line-off-line purchasing services, by connecting an internet payment network with a chain of stores. In 2016 Alibaba made an agreement with Walmart in the USA so that Chinese tourists and residents can use Alipay as a payment system.

As the Chinese market is already controlled by two leading companies, Alibaba and Tencent, foreign competitors are joining the fray. In late 2015, Apple and Samsung reached an agreement with China UnionPay (CUP), the first credit card payment network owned by the State banks, to develop a payment service using contactless prepaid cards using RFI (Radio frequency identification) and NFC (Near Field Communication) technology.

Online Banking

In June 2015, WeBank (Tencent's banking unit) and MyBank (Alibaba) were granted a full-fledged banking licence. E-banks' aim is to reach customers who have no access to the banking system. "*The Chinese financial industry, and in particular the banking industry, serves only 20% of the potential customers and thus 80% is not covered*" (Jack Ma).[3] "*500 million consumers who are making financial transactions … are not covered by the current financial system*" (Zane Wang).[4]

On the occasion of the opening ceremony of WeBank, a Shenzen-based 30% banking affiliate of Tencent (owner of WeChat, a social networking device), the Prime Minister Li Ke qian made a statement: "*We are going to lower the costs in favor of small customers, while making pressure on traditional financial institutions to accelerate the reforms … This is a small step for WeBank, but a giant one for the financial reform.*" By pushing a button, Li Ke qiang extended the first loan: a Rmb 35,000 ($5600) loan to a truck driver. The loans are designed for small borrowers (60% of the market) and the loan unit amount should not exceed Rmb 1 million ($154,000).

[3] *People's Daily*, the Party newspaper.

[4] Zane Wang, founder and CEO of China Rapid Finance, an online lending platform.

A few weeks later, Alibaba launched an online bank, MyBank, a joint venture between Ant Small & Micro Financial Services Group (Alibaba's financial affiliate) and Fosun, each owning 30% and 20% respectively.

In November, Baidu, a joint venture with Citic Bank, the bank affiliate of the State owned CITIC group, launched an online bank. Since then, three other non-banking institutions have been granted a banking licence: Shanghai Huarui Bank, Tianjin Jincheng Bank and Wenzhou Business Bank. All of them are located in the south-east coastal provinces, the richest and the most open to reforms, which are usually selected as the experimental sites. Lenovo (the world's second largest PC manufacturer) and the fast-growing smartphone manufacturer, Xiaomi, have applied to get a banking licence. ING, the Dutch bank, is in the process of negotiation with the Bank of Beijing, a regional bank owned by the local government, to create a joint online bank. According to ING, the default rate of credit in China is lower than in Europe.

Focusing on consumer's credit and lending to small companies, online banks have developed a new business model using new techniques of analysis and risk management. Thanks to customer databases (e-payment, social networks, online games), the e-banks affiliated to an internet group can make credit decisions within a short period of time. WeBank is using the customer data collection of WeChat's (Tencent) 600 million users. Online banks usually sub-contract the credit analysis to third-party companies which have developed highly sophisticated algorithms to establish the credit rating of each customer.[5] Tencent group has acquired China Rapid Finance, a rating company which has developed a programme that analyses the frequency of game playing and the time spent by customers on social networks and online games. Based upon this database, China Rapid Finance is in a situation to check a customer's borrowing behaviour. During a six-month experiment, China Rapid Finance came to the conclusion that the default rate is slightly above the default rate of credit card owners. The maturities and the amount may be limited, a minimum

[5] The government is supporting a research programme on borrower screening. The database collected by the online networks and banks can be used for other purposes such as health, education and employment, but also for more dubious purposes. According to government statements, the data collected by the e-bank could be used to select the "good" citizens, "honest, upright, lawful" and "credit worth" ones.

amount of Rmb 500 ($80) for a short period of time, but the rates are high: up to 21% on an annual basis.

Once the loan portfolio has grown, online banks plan to rebuild their lending capacity by selling the loans to asset management companies, investment funds specializing in asset management, and insurance companies in search of assets that match the maturity schedule of their liabilities. In 2014, Orient, one of the four defeasance companies who purchased the loan portfolios from the four "state banks", auctioned $2 billion's worth of credits that was eventually allocated to Citibank.

Banking regulation was amended to support the growth of e-banking. As the e-banks have not yet build up a customer deposit base, the solvency ratio which prohibits banks to lend over 75% of their deposits has been amended: some banks (small banks, online banks) are no longer subject to the lending ratio; and some types of credit that are targeted by e-banks (SMEs, rural firms) have been removed from the ratio. Also, the regulation on fraudulent loans which requires, among other things, that the lending contract should be signed by the borrower in the bank office, does not apply to online banks.[6]

Lending Platforms

Through a P2P (Peer-to-Peer) lending platform, investors and borrowers are in direct contact. The Chinese lending platforms started relatively early and have been growing very fast. From 2012 to 2016, the number of lending platforms increased 10 times from 40 to 4000. The lending platforms are not authorized to lend, but most of the lending platforms (95%) offer a guarantee (advanced payment) to the lenders. The guarantee scheme is managed by the lending platform through credit provisions

[6] The most frequent source of fraud relates to the borrower identity and the real worth of the collateralized assets. In 2014, the new Chairman of Bank of Lizhou (Sichuan) discovered that 40% of the bank's assets ($4.9 billion out of $80 billion total assets) were fraudulent. The fraudulent loans have been granted to one borrower, a businessman, via a member of his family, against worthless or non-existent collateral. According to the local press, the total loss reached $7.9 billion, i.e. eight times the annual bank profit. The big banks are also hit. In 2015, CITIC discovered that $147 billion of loans were granted against false bank acceptances, the proceeds being invested in securities. One week later, Agricultural Bank of China discovered $587 billion in fraudulent loans.

or sold to a third party such as a bank or an insurance company. An increasing number of lending platforms are providing the whole range of services (P2P): exchange, information, credit analysis, fund collection and repository, and guarantee (Fig. 7.2).

By the end of 2015, there were 2600 lending platforms with outstanding credit amounting to Rmb 439 billion ($66 billion). The lending platforms specializing in crowdfunding put together investors and borrowing companies in search of financing. They provide a better return to investors and an alternative source of credit to individuals and companies that have exhausted their borrowing capacity and have no access to bank credit.

The first Chinese lending platform, Credit Ease, was launched in 2006, soon followed by Paipad (Shanghai) in 2007. At about the same time Western lending platforms were launched: Online Lending Platform (UK) in 2005 and Prosper (USA) in 2006. In 2016, Credit Ease was the most important in terms of volume of transactions ($15 billion in 2015). In December 2015, Yirendai, Credit Ease's consumer credit department, was listed on the NASDAQ where it raised $75 million. In 2011, Ping

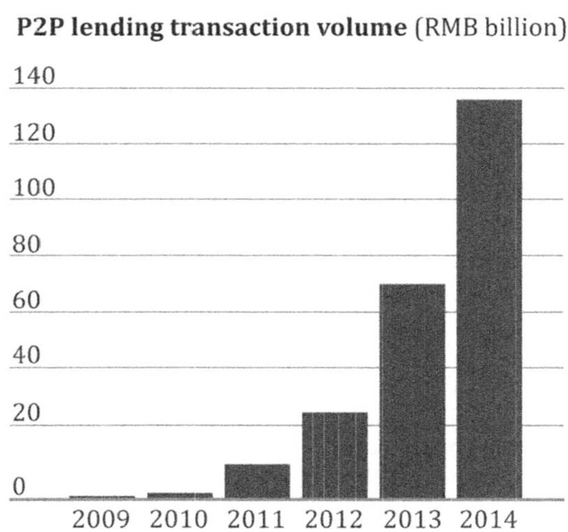

Fig. 7.2 P2P lending transaction volume
Source: IResearch report, 2014 forecast

An Insurance Company created Lufax (Shanghai Luijiazui International Financial Assets Exchange Co.), the first lending platform affiliated to a non-internet network company. Following the issue of capital funds from investors such as Bank of China, Guotai Junan Securities (Hong Kong) and Minsheng Bank, in 2015, Lufax's valuation reached $18.5 billion. Lufax is expected to get listed on the Shanghai and/or Hong Kong stock exchange in the course of 2016.

The lending platform often takes over loans that do not meet the bank's credit criteria and that are later sold to investors, mostly banks and asset management companies. Privately owned P2P lending platform Baozhi360 took over Rmb 99 billion ($15 billion) of non-redeemable loans. Zichan360 lending platform bought 59,000 problematic loans worth Rmb 1.5 billion ($200 million). It is said that 400 debt collection firms have been appointed to recover loans granted to 200 companies.

Now Chinese lending platforms are moving into the international arena. In 2016, Alibaba's largest lending platform launched a joint venture with America's largest one, the US Lending Club. Alibaba.com's e-Credit Line, managed by Lending Club, is offering credit within less than five minutes to American SMEs buying products made in China through Alibaba's networks. Loans granted by Lending Club are short-term credit (less than six months) of up to $300,000 at a rate of 0.5–2.4%, much lower than the one from Bank of China credit. Loans are sold to institutional investors. Jack Ma, Chairman of Alibaba, stated that the lending platform is targeting 2 billion customers and 10 million companies abroad. Lending Club is expecting to attract millions of Alibaba users. However, the problems experienced by Lending Club in late 2016 may jeopardize the development of this joint venture.

Online banking is not yet regulated although the death rate of e-banks is high and their lifetimes are short. In 2014, out of 900 lending platforms, 367 disappeared. On average every year the number of casualties amounts to 50% of new entrants. In 2015, the central bank undertook an enquiry into the framework of a regulation. As a first step, PBOC noticed that over 10 government bodies are involved one way or another in lending platform regulation and supervision.

The Chinese government is actively supporting the development of new banking techniques and new banking institutions with the aim of lowering the borrowing costs of the most sensitive industries, extending credit facilities to small companies that have no access to bank credit, and increasing competition in the banking sector. Some Chinese analysts think that the traditional State and commercial banks have already lost the "digital war".

References

1. Wang, Jiazhuo G., Hongwei Xu, and Jun Ma. eds. 2015. *Financing the Underfinanced: Online Lending in China*. New York: Springer.
2. McLuhan, Marshall. 2008. *The Medium is the Message: An Inventory of Effects*. London: Penguin Classics.

8

Government Controlled Financial Institutions

The emergence of financial markets is the latest step in the on-going policy of reform and opening up. The development of a financial asset market was the key prerequisite for the proper running of the other production factors' markets: the market for goods and services as well as the labour market. But it was also the apex of the struggle between "reformists" supporting the growing implementation of market mechanisms, and "conservatives" supporting the role of the State. Economic reform is a mix of ideological postures. In fact, this typically Western-minded dichotomy is meaningless in China: most of the high-ranking Chinese Communist Party (CCP) officials are both "reformists" in the economic field and "conservatives" in the political sphere. Above all, the Chinese leaders have a very pragmatic approach: what makes the economic system work best? What are the economic reforms compatible with the Party-State's leadership?

The Chinese "Big Bang" involves the government in an area which so far has remained mostly chaotic and disorganized, spanning the grey area between full authorization and formal ban. Banks opened a "secondary" bond market by buying back treasury bonds before maturity. Local authorities are selling "municipal" bonds through the banking networks

D. De Rambures, F. Escobar Duenas, *China's Financial System*,
DOI 10.1007/978-3-319-40451-6_8

to finance off-budget investments and infrastructures. Local banks are trading these "municipal" bonds. Experimental exchanges arose in the Special Economic Area (Shenzen, Shanghai) to supply financing to local companies. The first commodity market was born in 1986 in Shenyang (Manchuria). The raw materials produced in this area, namely oil and coal, are listed. Other commodity exchanges followed suit with other commodities (cotton, pork and soy) and other markets (Shanghai and Zhengzou). The stock markets followed the same pattern. In November 1984, Shanghaî Fei Lo Acoustics Corp. sold Rmb 500,000 shares on the Shangaî exchange through a "private" placement at a price set by a pool of underwriters. In January 1985 the first public offering took place: Shanghaî Industrial managed to sell stocks. The offering price, set by the administration, was unrelated to the market price since there was no market, but the sale was backed by a repurchase option from the issuing banks.

In 1990–1991 the government stepped into the field and reorganized the so far disorganized and unofficial markets. All the local exchanges were closed (Wuhan, Shenyang, Tianjin, Chongking…), and the transactions collated into two stock markets—Shanghai and Shenzen—plus a third one, Hong Kong, when the city reverted to China in 1997. Shanghai is the largest financial centre and in the heart of the most dynamic area; Shenzen is an Experimental Economic Area, the shop window of the regime; and Hong Kong is the connection with the outside world.

Following the Asian crisis (1997), China reinforced its financial regulation of the financial industry: banks, insurance companies and investment companies (trusts). In 1998 the "Security Law" dealt with the security of transactions; in 1998 the "Investment Fund Law" defined the legal status of public saving institutions; in 1999 a new supervisory agency was created, CSRC (China Securities Regulatory Commission). Two competing institutions—the central banks' PBOC and the supervision agency CSRC, both of them reporting to the State Council—are in charge of regulation and supervision.

After building up the legal background, the government imposed a set of measures to improve the market's liquidity. In 2001, under the leadership of the then Prime Minister, Zhu Rong ji, the State Council gave instructions to sell 10% of the SOE (State Owned Enterprise) non-negotiable A shares. In 2002, according to the new market regulations, banks, insurance companies, investment funds and pension funds such as the NSSF (National Social Security Fund) had access to the stock markets. In 2003, QFII (Qualified Foreign Institutional Investor) licences were granted to a handful of foreign banks that are authorized to trade the Chinese yuan's denominated securities. RQFII (Renminbi Qualified Foreign Institutional Investor) licences were granted to Hong Kong-based joint ventures between Chinese banks and foreign banks.

Now that a stock market was operating, the government was in a position to start an ambitious wave of "privatization" to provide the "offer" side of the market. State owned banks and companies were listed on the Stock Exchange. In 2012, a new team of rulers had reached power led by Hu Jin tao and Wen Jia bao. Hu is said to be more "State" oriented, while Wen is supposed to be more "market" friendly. This is a traditional "division of labour" between the two heads of government. The Prime Minister, in charge of economic policy, is expected to be more open to reforms. The President of the Republic and Party Secretary, who has been entrusted with the political and social stability, is expected to be more "statist" and "conservative".

Regulation and Supervision

In developed countries, there are two kinds of supervision schemes: a "sectorial" approach, such as the American SEC (Securities and Exchange Commission); and a "global" approach, such as the British FSA (Financial Supervision Agency) with extended powers. The FSA was created in the aftermath of the 2008 financial crisis, precisely with the aim of having a wider scope of responsibility. Both organizations are independent of the government, just like the central bank. The Chinese supervision agency follows neither approach: even though its field of operation is limited to the financial markets, its range of powers is very large, but it is highly dependent from the government. Like all the Chinese government supervision bodies, the CSRC reports to the State Council.

The CSRC is in charge of the regulation of markets and the supervision of financial institutions. Key decisions are taken by the State Council and implemented by the CSRC. Every call to public saving (listing on the stock exchange, bond issue, capital increase, mergers and acquisitions) is screened by the CSRC and authorized under certain conditions. There is no recourse against its decisions. In case of public offerings, the CSRC gets into the detail: the amount of the transaction, the percentage of shares sold (float) and the listing market. When it comes to simultaneous issues both on the Shanghai and Hong Kong exchanges, as is often the case, the share of each market is analyzed in detail: the distribution between institutional investors and individual savers, the offering price, the allocation of shares, the leading banks, the underwriting group and all other provisions (such as the lock up clause and the green shoe clause).[1] According to a 2015 State Council decision, the CSRC's power is no longer arbitrary and should be restricted to checking compliance with legal provisions. Up to now, as experienced during the 2015 stock crisis, nothing has changed.

The State Council represents the only possible arbitrage level between the central bank and the supervision agency, because both of them report to it. Every "technical" issue becomes *de facto* a "political" issue. In theory, the central bank is in charge of financial stability while the CSRC is in charge of regulation and supervision of security markets. But monetary policy and regulation of financial markets are closely tied up. If the interest rate goes down, financial markets move up and vice versa. The purchase of securities is financed through banking credit. If the borrowing cost goes up, security dealing goes down. In such a case, reimbursing bank loans may be detrimental to stock dealers and traders, stock trading companies, investment funds, mutual funds, hedging funds and individual savers.

Following the 2015 stock crisis, Xiao Gang, the CSRC manager appointed in 2003, was dismissed and replaced by Li Shi yu, then Chairman of ABC (Agricultural Bank of China) and a former vice Chairman of the central bank. Once again the very "political" and well-connected Zhu Xiao chuan, Chairman of PBOC for over 13 years, managed to save his position. This is a sign of the growing weight of monetary policy and the central bank in the implementation of economic policy.

---

[1] According to the "lock up" clause, the shareholders are prohibited from selling their shares within a given period of time (from six months to three years), to prevent a fall in the stock price shortly after the issue; the "green shoe" clause authorizes an increase of the transaction amount in case the issue is oversubscribed.

The development of financial markets is not only a matter of volume of transactions and market capitalization, but also and more importantly a matter of expertise. The Chinese markets have developed the whole range of trading infrastructure. Delivery versus Payment (DVP) techniques that are processing transactions are strong enough to absorb occasional peaks, quick enough to process transactions in real time, and sound enough to ensure that both legs of the deals are properly matched. The current operating system is able to prevent the spread of risk (liquidity risk, counterparty risk, market risk, etc.)[2] to other markets.

The whole range of financial institutions is now available: investment banks, investment funds, security brokers, institutional investors, asset management companies, private equity funds, etc. Initially, most of these market participants had been built up in partnership, with Western companies providing the expertise while the Chinese partner provided the customer base, the selling capacity and above all the market knowledge and connections with the right people within government administrations. As soon as the Chinese institutions had full control over the technology, foreign partners were pushed aside to new fields of operation, and so on. In the fully competitive areas, foreign banks are pushed onto the sidelines and kept in a marginal position.

Investment Banks

Investment banks are matching companies' and investors' financial needs: companies are in search of financing and investors are in search of investment opportunities that fit their needs. Covering the whole range of financial services—company listing, security brokerage, asset management, commodity trading, mergers and acquisitions, etc.—investment banks are indispensable in balancing market forces. Their profits are mainly owed to fees, but to serve their clients they have to take positions. Thanks to the leverage effect and the high turnover of their positions, investment banks are usually very profitable ventures.

[2] Liquidity risk arises when either cash or securities are no longer available; the counterparty risk when one of the two deal makers failed in the course of the transaction and cannot meet its side of the deal.

Originally, most Chinese investment banks were formed as joint ventures with foreign banks. As the market was growing and diversifying, the leading Chinese investment banks managed to buy back the shares of foreign banks. CITIC took over Banco de Bilbao's stake, CICC bought back Morgan Stanley's stake and so on. In most cases participation was acquired by Chinese investors: insurance companies, sovereign funds, State owned banks, and by foreign investors confined to being sleeping partners, simply looking for profits, dividends and capital gains when their participations were sold out to the market. However, in China there is no Chinese wall between commercial banking and investment banking. CITIC has created an affiliated commercial bank, CITIC Bank, which is listed on the Hong Kong Exchange (Figs. 8.1 and 8.2).

The leading investment banks are CITIC, a wholly owned government bank, and CICC (China International Capital Corp.), an affiliated bank of CCB (China Construction Bank), one of the four State banks, and the second largest Chinese bank. The most profitable are CITIC, IBOC

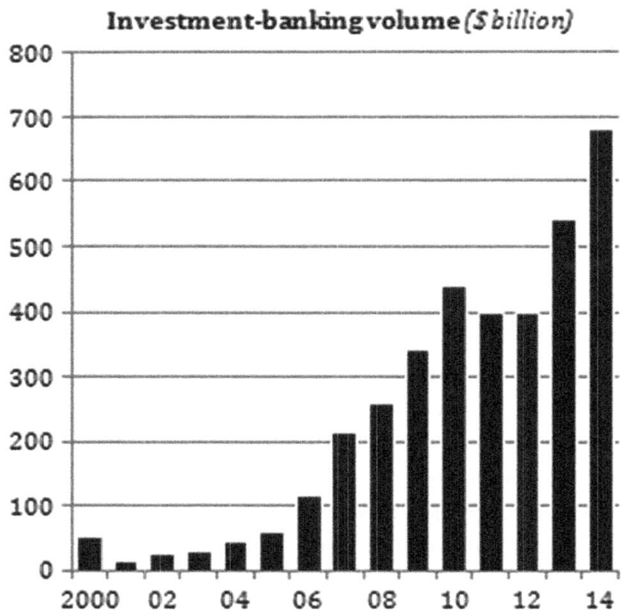

Fig. 8.1 Investment banking volume
Source: Thomson Reuters

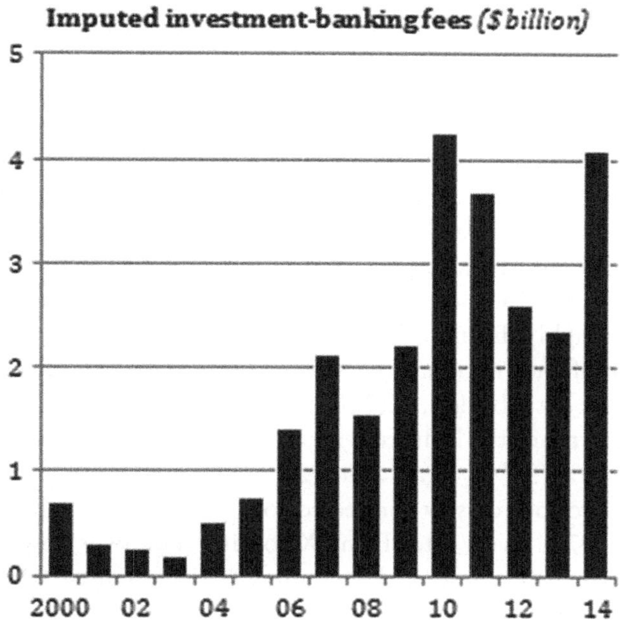

Fig. 8.2 Imputed investment banking fees
Source: The *Wall Street Journal*

(International Bank of China), an affiliate of BOC (Bank of China), and GUOSEN Securities, a brokerage firm that turned to investment banking.

CITIC

CITIC Group (China International Trust and Investment Corp.), a State owned bank, holds a dominant position in the investment banking market, being awarded most of the mandates. Due to its market share and government connections, nothing can be done without its consent. CITIC plays a key role in government policy. Like CDB (China Development Bank), CITIC is the government arm in every financing package raised in favour of domestic as well as foreign policy objectives. Due to its close connection with the government, CITIC involvement in a deal is a sign of the government's interest. In 2016, for financing the aborting acquisition of Syntega, the Swiss agro-business group by ChemChina (China National Chemical Corp), CITIC got a mandate to put together a three-month $15 billion bridge financing deal to ChemChina, while Citic Bank for the domestic tranche and HSBC for the international tranche managed a $5 billion loan. Allocating the mandate for such a big deal to such a small bank was surprising, but the appointment was indicative.

CITIC Group has a dominant market share in every market area: project financing, stock public offering, mergers and acquisitions, stock trading, commodity trading, real estate, asset management, and so on. CITIC is a highly diversified investment bank and a major international player, one of the "national champions" backed by the government. In term of asset distribution, CITIC invested primarily in infrastructures (84%). In terms of the industrial sector, it invested mainly in three areas: Iron and Metal (33%), Real Estate (23%) and Steel (22%).[3]

CITIC Group is closely connected to the ruling class. The Group was created in 1979, a year after Deng Xiao ping took over power, by Rong Yi ren (1916–2005), one of the very few "red capitalists" who stayed in Mainland China in 1949. In the 1930s, Rong's father was the wealthiest man in China and a paragon of wild capitalism. A victim of the Cultural Revolution (1966–1976), Rong Yi ren was the PRC (People's Republic of China) Vice President (1993–1997). CITIC is one of the "TIC" (Trust and Investment Companies)[4] reporting direct to the State Council. CITIC has long been chaired by Jiang Zhen min, son of former President and Party Secretary, Jiang Ze min (1989–2003), the leader of the Shanghai faction, who, despite being 90 years old, is still enjoying an influential position within the Party.

In 2006, BBVA (Banco de Bilbao Viscaya Argentaria) took a 4.83% stake in CITIC with an option to raise its participation to 15%. Also, BBVA took a 15% participation in CITIC's international affiliate, Citic International Financing, with an option to raise its participation to 30%, totalling $1.8 billion. BBVA is strongly established in Latin America, a source of critical raw material for Chinese industry; in exchange, BBVA could expect to penetrate the Chinese market through its CITIC partnership. Now China

[3] Financial Times/Goldman Sachs, 2014.

[4] Formed in 1999 after the same model, GITIC (Guangdong International Trust & Investment Corp.) based in Guangzhou (Canton) was closed following huge losses on the London futures market.

is well established in South America, while CITIC is leading the investment banking market in China. Hit by the world's financial crisis, BBVA had to focus on its core business and sell back its participation in 2013 (now down to 5.1%). In 2015, on the occasion of the CITIC listing on the Hong Kong Stock Exchange, CITIC sold a 20% participation to the Japanese trading company, Itochu, and the Thai food company, CP Group (Chaoren Pokphand), two shareholders who are not going to interfere in the bank's management.

The same misfortune befell Crédit Agricole. CITIC took a participation in CLSA, a very successful investment bank based in Hong Kong with offices on the Mainland. Originally, Crédit Agricole expected to form a worldwide investment bank along with CITIC and the stock broker, Chevreux. Step by step, CITIC participation was raised until 2013 when Crédit Agricole sold its remaining stake.

In the meantime, CITIC was restructuring the whole group. In 2014, CITIC Pacific, the loss-originating Hong Kong affiliate, renamed CITIC Ltd., made two capital increases: $29 billion entirely subscribed by the parent company, and $8 billion subscribed by State enterprises such as NSSF (National Social Security Fund). The proceeds of the capital increase were used to finance the acquisition of CITIC Holding assets to reshape the loss-originating CITIC Pacific. By the end of the process, CITIC Ltd. (ex-CITIC Pacific) was controlled up to 58% by CITIC Holding, while the latter was 83% owned by the government. On the one hand, now the CITIC listing on the Hong Kong Stock Exchange was compelled to disclose critical information, but on the other hand the CITIC Group had a vehicle to tap the foreign market without threatening ultimate State control.

CITIC's financing is at the crossroads of politics and business. CITIC is often requested to extend huge dollar-denominated financing to State owned companies such as Sinochem (chemical, fertilizers, petroleum) to back their international development and take advantage of borrowing at a low interest rate of a weakening currency. In 2015, CITIC placed on the Hong Kong market a $6 billion loan to the food producer Shaunghui (a meat producer) to finance the acquisition of the American pork producer, Smithfield Foods. Pork meat being the basic food of all Chinese families, the control of pork supply is a highly strategic industry.

Due to its close connections with the government, CITIC may be requested to get involved in the financing of more political- than business-related projects. In 2008, CITIC opened the world's largest iron mine in Australia to supply the iron-consuming Chinese industries. Following the yuan revaluation (up to 2015), CITIC's investment entailed huge foreign exchange losses on top of the industrial losses owing to the fall of iron and steel prices on the world market. In 2014, CITIC Pacific made a deal with an Indian group, the over-indebted Amil Ambani, on the verge of bankruptcy, to create a joint venture between CITIC Telecom and Ambani's affiliate, Reliance Communications, in the very strategic area of underwater cables.

CICC

In 1995 the investment bank CICC (China International Capital Corp.) was funded through a partnership between the State bank CCB (China Construction Bank) and Morgan Stanley who took a 34.3% stake along with a group of investors including China Jianyin Investment Ltd., CNIGC (China National Investment & Guarantee Co. Ltd.), SIC (Government of Singapore Investment Corp.), a Singaporean sovereign wealth fund, and Mingly Corp., an affiliate of CHA, a Hong Kong-based metal trading company. In 2010, Morgan Stanley was forced to resell 20% to two US investment companies: KKR (Kohlberg Kravis Robert) and Blackstone. In 2016, CICC was controlled up to 44% by China's sovereign fund, CIC (China Investment Fund), 16% by GIC and 20% by the two US investment funds (10% each).[5]

However, in spite of the above-mentioned misfortunes, most of the prominent investment banks are established on the Chinese market through minority shareholdings in Chinese joint ventures (Table 8.1).

[5] Following the 2015 crash of the Chinese stock market, both funds are forbidden to sell off their shares.

Table 8.1 Foreign investment banks in China

Morgan Stanley	Huaxin Securities (2011)
JP Morgan	First Capital Securities (2011)
BNP Paribas	Changjiang Securities Corp. Ltd. (33%) (2002–2007)
Goldman Sachs	Gaohua Securities (33%) (2004)
Citigroup	Central China Securities (2008)
Credit Suisse	Founder Securities (2008)
Deutsche Bank	Shanxi Securities (Zhong De Securities) (2009)
UBS	Beijing Securities (2006)
Royal Bank of Scotland	Huaying Securities (2011)

Investment Funds

Chinese financial markets are very volatile. This is due among other things to the lack of institutional investors that accounts for only 50% of the volume (against 80% in the USA) and 25% of the transactions, in spite of a fast-growing volume of transactions. The number of investment funds (mutual funds, hedge funds) has increased from 95 in 2003 to 1552 in 2013. Over the same period of time, the volume of assets managed by investment funds rose from Rmb 16 billion ($2.5 billion) to Rmb 311 billion ($50 billion). In this regard China ranks third in Asia behind Japan and Australia. Investment funds have a mere 7% share of the $7000 billion Chinese savings (2013), far behind the market share of the UK investment funds (17%) and the US ones (38%). Chinese investment funds account for half of the total assets owned by Chinese institutional investors, i.e. 25% of total financial assets. The asset portfolio of investment funds is comparable in terms of magnitude to the one from insurance companies. However, China has developed a variety of investment funds: hedge funds, mutual funds, pension funds, equity funds, sovereign funds, ETFs (Exchange Traded Funds), trackers, index funds, etc.

Legal Framework

In 1991, the supervision body, CSRC (China Securities Recovery Commission, which was still a department of the central bank), issued a directive regulating investment funds (*Provisory Measures for the Administration of Investment Funds in Securities*) according to which: all funds must be registered and authorized by the CSRC, minimum paid capital is Rmb 300 millions ($45 millions) with a five-year management contract, all capital increases should be authorized by the CSRC, and a minimum 20% of investment fund assets should be invested in government bonds.

In 1998, CSRC authorized five closed investment funds (fixed capital)—Jintai, Kaiyun, Xinghua, Anxin and Yuyang—along with five asset management companies. The shares were booked in security accounts held by the banks. In 2000, CSRC issued a new directive concerning open funds (floating capital) (*Pilot Measures for Open Ended Securities Investment Funds*) which were now accounting for up to 95% of the investment funds.

To increase the liquidity of the market, the CSRC kept widening the range of investment funds. In 2006, the pension funds were launched. Most of them are actually foreign funds marketed by Chinese banks to their customers. However, 29 licences were granted to such banks as ICBC, BOCOM, Shanghai Pudong Development Bank, China Merchant Bank and China Everbright. In 2007, 13 "Morningstar" funds using graphic management techniques were marketed. Morgan Stanley started a MSCI index (Morgan Stanley Commodity Index) which led to the floating of ETFs. In 2007, the year before the crisis erupted, the value of Chinese funds jumped to 162%. Some of them doubled, such as JP China A (JP Morgan) investing in A shares, Fidelity Fund China Focus (Fidelity Investment Luxembourg), Invesco PRC Equity A (Invesco Asset Management Ireland Ltd), Saint Honoré Chine (Compagnie Financière Edmond de Rotschild) and Dexia Equity B Red Chips C (Dexia Management).[6]

The 2008 financial crisis did not stop market growth. The stock index fell from 6000 down to 2000 within a year (October 2007–October

[6] A shares are yuan denominated shares sold to the Chinese; B shares used to be yuan denominated shares which could paid in foreign currency; C shares are the Blue Chips quoted on a foreign exchange, mostly on the New York Stock Exchange.

2008), as the volume of transactions plummeted from $138 billion (June 2007) down to $28 billion (August 2008). Even while the volume of assets managed by the funds fell from 32.84% of the stock exchange capitalization (Shanghai plus Shenzen) in December 2007 down to 9.70% in December 2011, the number of new funds doubled, but this was more than compensated for by the closing of an equivalent amount of funds. The short lives of Chinese funds is owed to the fee structures: as opposed to Western funds, the front end fees of Chinese funds are higher and the annual fees lower, so it is in the banks' and brokers' interest to sell new funds rather than old ones. In order to correct the bias owed to the fee structure, CSRC gave a licence to four "independent" (non-banking) brokerage firms to market their own funds, with the aim of creating customer loyalty over the long term.

To further increase market liquidity, the Chinese government authorized foreign funds to market yuan denominated funds on the domestic market. In 2011, seven Yuan denominated funds managed by foreign funds were launched including Goldman Sachs, Morgan Stanley, Carlyle, Blackstone and TPG. Sometimes equity funds are created upon the initiative of local authorities to attract foreign investment. The City of Beijing funded two equity funds in partnership with foreign investors (Carlyle and Goldman Sachs) to take a stake in local companies, thus contributing to the economic development of the area.

In 2013, the government authorized the launching of funds specialized in overseas investments. Six foreign funds were allowed to raise $50 million each on the domestic market to be invested in foreign securities: Canyon Partners (Los Angeles), Citadel (Chicago), Man Group (London, the largest European fund), Oaktree (USA), Och-Ziff (USA) and Winton Capital (the largest fund using graphic analysis).

In spite of market fluctuations, a great number of Chinese funds managed to make a gain on both sides, from the volume of funds collected and from the increased value of the investment. Hill House Capital, a Shanghai-based fund, launched in 2005 with a capital base of $30 million, managed a $6 billion portfolio in 2012. Prime Capital Management (Shanghai), created in 2003 and which was managing over $3 billion, had produced an average profit of 26% over its first 10 years. In 2014, Prime Capital launched a fund on the Hong Kong market which had collected over $4 billion within a year.[7] In 2013, two Chinese funds, namely China Asset Management ($50.5 billion) and Harvest Fund Management ($48.8 billion), managed to reach the world's 200 largest funds (Fig. 8.3).

However, the Chinese fund industry is concentrated on a limited number of funds. Out of 80 funds, 20 are responsible for half of the total capitalization. A dozen funds have only an asset portfolio over Rmb 3 billion ($450 million).

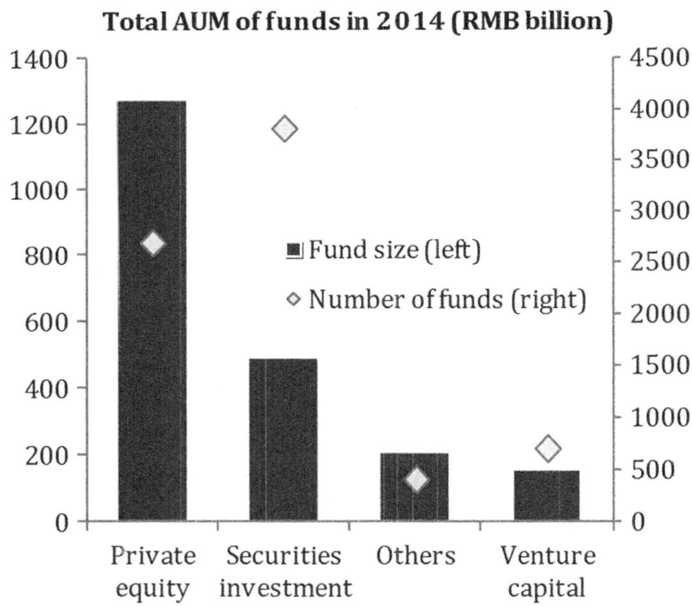

Fig. 8.3 Total AUM of funds in 2014

[7] Prime Capital is headed by a former futures dealer from the private equity fund Yangjin.

Sovereign Wealth Funds

Among the 10 largest sovereign wealth funds (SWFs) in the world, five are Chinese: CIC (China Investment Fund) (third), SAFE (State Agency of Foreign Exchange) (fourth), HKMA (Hong Kong Monetary Authority) (seventh) and NSSF (National Social Security Fund) (ninth). The Chinese SWFs share the same objectives as the other sovereign funds: increase the return of foreign exchange reserves, finance infrastructure projects and fund pension schemes. However, the Chinese SWFs have some objectives of their own: to prevent the inflationary impact of foreign exchange inflows, to back the acquisitions of foreign companies by Chinese companies, and more generally, to support China's foreign policy.

The volume of foreign exchange holdings exceeds by far the needs of Chinese industry: foreign exchange reserves amount to 37.5% of GDP while imports amount to 23% of GDP. In spite of huge outflows ($1 billion in 2015 following the combined foreign exchange and stock exchange crisis), the volume of foreign exchange covers more than one year's worth of imports, as a volume amounting to two to three months' worth of imports is found reasonable. The final objective of having huge foreign exchange reserves is more political than economic. It is part of the policy of reform and opening up. The cushion of foreign exchange reserves gives the Chinese leader a priceless asset: time.

Foreign exchange reserves were piled up to keep the Chinese economy protected from outside shocks during the implementation of the transition policy and its late impact.

In the early days of the reform policy, the government was focusing on public investments and infrastructures, indispensable to economic growth, but which were not liable to private investment due to low and very long-term returns. This policy was relying on competitive exports of mass consumption products. The sale of mass consumption products and the accumulation of foreign exchange reserves were aimed at financing the purchase of capital equipment.

The XIIth (2011–2016) and the XIIIth (2017–2023) five-year plans put the emphasis on the transition from an investment and export-led growth engine to a consumption, services and innovation-led growth one. As a result, over the last five years, household income increased on average by 13% per year. In the meantime, Chinese industry was relying on foreign demand until the development of domestic demand was able to meet the increased consumption needs.

With a view of taming the inflationary effect of an accumulation of foreign reserves, the government had neutralized the inflow of foreign currency by promoting the acquisition of foreign assets: either financial assets or industrial assets. The foreign currency earned through commercial and investment surpluses was normally stockpiled in PBOC vaults in exchange for yuan. In order to freeze the proceeds of the yuan created through the sale of foreign currency, the central bank issued "financial bills" to mop up excess liquidity. Otherwise, the foreign currency assets were used to buy US Treasury Bonds and/or purchase foreign companies as a follow up to the growing internationalization of Chinese industry. As long as the yuan was rising against the US dollar, these dollar denominated assets were a source of foreign exchange losses. When the dollar rose, the dollar denominated assets were a shield against adverse movements of exchange rates.

China Investment Corp

Created in 2003, CIC (China Investment Corp.) reports directly to the State Council. CIC has a $700 billion worth asset portfolio. Every year $300 billion of additional funds are allocated to CIC. In 2015 the huge losses experienced in foreign exchange reserves changed the situation: it is likely that the volume of foreign exchange reserves allocated to CIC by the Central Bank (SAFE) may be revised downward.

Usually foreign media put the emphasis on CIC's acquisitions abroad. In fact, CIC is mostly active in the domestic market: out of $700 billion assets, $500 billion is invested in Chinese ventures. In theory, CIC is a mere investment vehicle and is not supposed to interfere in the management of affiliated companies. According to Li Jin qin, Chairman of the Board, CIC is not expected to take a controlling interest in foreign companies. Usually, CIC's shareholdings do not exceed 5–10% of the capital. However, CIC is supporting China's foreign policy more broadly, playing a key role in the financing packages granted to foreign countries in order

Table 8.2 Geographic distribution of CIC shareholding (%)

North America	43.8%
Asia Pacific	29.6%
Europe	20.6%
Latin America	4.7%
Africa	1.3%

Source: CIC annual report (2012)

to facilitate the completion of a deal. Also, it appears that CIC teams up with a Chinese company to increase the weight of Chinese interests and the government's control in a sensitive foreign acquisition.

In geographic and industrial terms, the distribution of CIC's assets fits with the order of priorities set by the government (Table 8.2).

Firstly, CIC is securing access to neighbouring markets. China's balance of trade is hugely positive with the USA and the European Union, but it is negative with its neighbouring countries. In addition, CIC is massively investing in south-east countries. Due to the wage increases in China over the last few years, a number of Chinese firms moved their manufacturing units to neighbouring low-labour cost countries: Vietnam, Thailand, Cambodia, Laos, Burma, Indonesia and the Philippines. In so doing, China is developing in South East Asia in the twenty-first century what the UK did in the nineteenth and what the USA did in the twentieth century all over the world: net inflows of foreign incomes (foreign investments) more than compensate for the net outflows of the trade balance. In 2015, for the first time, Chinese investments abroad ($145.7 billion) overtook foreign investments in China ($135.6 billion).

CIC's investment policy is concentrated on access to raw materials desperately needed by the thirsty Chinese manufacturing engine, within a policy of construction of infrastructure against the delivery of raw material. Most of extraction fields in under-developed countries demand huge investments in infrastructure (refinery plants, road or railway access to the site, sea or railway terminals, storage facilities) which the local government is not able to finance. Such infrastructure linked to development sites requires substantial and diversified financing packages including different sources of funds. Quite often CIC plays a critical role along with Chinese companies and policy banks in joint ventures with local mining companies.

Now CIC is focusing on access to Western technology. When Western companies were out of reach, CIC turned to the sub-contractors of critical businesses such as car manufacturing, aircraft industry, aerospace suppliers, fintech and more generally high-tech firms that were developing new products, new techniques or new processes. In Europe, the bulk of Chinese investment is concentrated in the UK (real estate, finance) and Germany (machine tools, robots). Volvo and its Chinese shareholder, Geely (Zheijiang Geely Holding Group), have designed an automated bus that, in April 2016, has been running without a driver for 35 km between two Chinese cities. Now CIC is putting the emphasis on distribution networks and brand acquisition in developed countries. CIC's portfolio is increasingly diversified. As an example, CIC has taken an €800 million shareholding in APAX, one of the largest European equity funds (€11.2 billion assets) (Table 8.3).

The asset distribution mirrors CIC's growing expertise in investment policy. The percentage of listed shares increased as compared to bonds and cash. CIC has hired the most knowledgeable experts and is resorting to the most sophisticated investment schemes and management techniques.

Following the lead of the Norwegian sovereign fund, the Government Pension Fund of Norway, it might be possible that CIC could split its asset portfolio between a domestic fund and an overseas fund, between a fund investing in industrial ventures, and a fund investing in financial assets.

In the long term, due to an increased average life expectancy, CIC will be involved in the yet to be formed national pension scheme.

Table 8.3 CIC's international asset distribution (%)

	2011	2012	2013
Listed shares	25%	32%	40.4%
Long-term investment[a]	31%	32.4%	28.2%
Bonds	21%	19.1%	17%
Hedge funds	12%	12.7%	11.8%
Cash	11%	3.8%	2.6%

Source: CIC annual report, 2014
[a]Real estate, infrastructures

On top of CIC, several other government investment funds, such as SAFE, the central bank department in charge of foreign exchange management, and NSSF (National Social Security Fund) in charge of social security contributions management, are also involved in the financial market and sometimes in the industrial shareholding sphere as well.

SAFE (State Agency of Foreign Exchange), a PBOC department,[8] is in charge of foreign exchange reserve management. Initially SAFE's investment policy was restricted to short-term highly liquid investments such as dollar denominated US Treasury Bonds. SAFE used to rely on professional asset managers. In 2008, after an auction, SAFE had allocated a $2.5 billion portfolio to TPG Capital (ex-Texas Pacific Group), which cost $1 billion in losses following the bankruptcy of the US bank, Washington Mutual. Following the fall in interest rates and average investment returns, SAFE got reorganized and more professional, hiring experienced traders and practising sophisticated management techniques. As the rate of return was steadily decreasing, SAFE had to disinvest to increase its share of more risky investments. In 2011, SAFE took a 3% participation in Munich Re, the world's largest insurance company.[9] In 2012, it took over the share portfolio of General Motors pension fund, through a $1.5 billion to $2 billion transaction (the figure was not disclosed). This is far greater than the usual investments of foreign exchange in liquid assets.

More surprising, in 2015, PBOC took a 3% participation in Mediobanca, an Italian group involved in industrial as well as in financial ventures, far from what was usually the role of a central bank. At that time it was said that Zhu Xiao chuan, the powerful PBOC governor, was considering building an investment fund to take advantage of the alternative investments which accounted for 17% of SAFE's assets, as compared to an average of 33% share of traditional hedge fund asset portfolios. Whatever the idea was in the back of his mind, such an investment was far from the prudent foreign exchange management expected from a central bank.

Like all of the other sovereign wealth funds, the impact of the Chinese funds is hard to assess. On the one hand, sovereign fund investments

[8] Zhu Xiao chuan, the current PBOC governor, used to be the head of SAFE.

[9] Along with a 10% shareholding by Warren Buffett's Berkshire Hathaway fund.

increase market liquidity and effectiveness. Like other institutional investors, but backed by a much stronger strike force, the sovereign investment funds can back stock prices in case of a crisis. CIC's investments are contributing substantially to the narrow stock markets of emerging countries. On the other hand, in contrast to the Norwegian sovereign fund, the Chinese sovereign funds do not disclose their investment policy and the distribution of their stock portfolio. In addition, due to the magnitude of funds available, sovereign funds' intervention in a market may entail wide fluctuations, especially in emerging markets.

Pension Funds

The insurance industry is usually split into two areas: life insurance and non-life insurance. Until recently (2015) non-life insurance, which is much more rewarding,[10] was out of the reach of foreign insurance companies. The volume of life insurance premiums is increasing fast, but the market coverage is still very limited and uneven. The product range is limited (life insurance policies). The management techniques (actuary) are relatively unknown. The hedging instruments, such as long-term bonds, are under-developed. The geographical market coverage is still restricted to cities: 50% of the urban population is covered as opposed to 10% of the rural population. The Chinese insurance sector is also very concentrated. A handful of State owned insurance companies have an overwhelming market share—PICC (38%), Ping An (15%), China Life (8.9%)—which is detrimental to competition and innovation. Through foreign acquisitions, insurance groups are increasingly becoming international. However, the bankruptcy of Fortis, the ailing Franco-Belgian banking group in which Ping An took a 5% stake, thus becoming the largest shareholder, has discouraged foreign acquisitions. Nonetheless, Chinese insurance companies are playing a key role in domestic financial markets, although not as big as it should be (Table 8.4).

[10] The car insurance department of PICC Property & Casualty Co. was providing 80% of the company's profits. From then on, foreign companies have access to the non-life insurance sector, but only within the framework of a 49% joint venture with a Chinese partner.

For years the government has been thinking about a State nationwide pension scheme. Today, rural workers have a monthly pension of a few dollars (not including the sale of their land lease). Following the 1997 law which authorized pensions funds, in most of the cities of the eastern and south-eastern provinces, companies' and local governments' pension schemes were funded by both employers' and employees' contributions. In the cities and the coastal provinces, all labour contracts include a provision regarding pension benefits. In China there are three pension systems: the government one (NSSF), the instalment one (EA) managed by companies, and pension funds managed by insurance companies (Table 8.5).

Created in 2000, the NSSF (National Social Security Fund), the social security fund which collects all the premiums, including pension

Table 8.4 Insurance company premiums

	Rmb mds	$ m
Non-life insurance	4026	643
Life insurance	10,501	1587
Life insurance	9679	1539
Health insurance	631	100
Other	189	30
Total	14,528	2306

Source: CIRC annual report 2014

Table 8.5 Assets portfolio of Chinese insurance companies (Rmb billion)

	Non-life insurance	Life insurance	Reinsurance	Chinese companies	Foreign companies	Total
2002	948	5161	211			6320
2003	1176	7657	255			9088
2004	1411	8352	262	11,540	413	11,953
2005	1718	13,458	292	14,630	660	15,286
2006	2340	17,446	311	18,862	862	19,704
2007	3880	23,249	877	27,656	1256	28,912
2008	4687	27,138	994	31,893	1524	33,418
2009	4892	33,655	1162	38,582	2052	40,634
2010	5833	42,642	1151	47,860	2621	50,481
2011	7919	49,798	1579	56,822	3006	59,828

Source: NBSC annual report 2014

contributions, is managed by NCSSF (National Council Social Security Fund). Initially, in accordance with government regulation, NSSF investment policy was restricted to yuan denominated Treasury Bonds. In 2014, NSSF was authorized to buy foreign stocks denominated in a foreign currency within some limits. NSSF foreign investment was made of US$ denominated stocks up to 80% and 20% of European stocks. Every two years, through a bidding process, NSSF reallocates the management of asset tranches to Chinese asset management firms such as China AM, Bosera and E. Fund Management, and to former defeasance companies converted into asset management firms such as Orient, Cindra and Great Wall. On the occasion of the 2012 auction, foreign asset management companies such as Fidelity had been allowed to join the bidding through joint ventures with Chinese partners (banks and insurance companies). In return NSSF was increasingly selling its management expertise. In 2012, NSSF took over the management of the pension fund of the (south-east) Guangdong province. As with other sovereign funds and development banks, NSSF is sometimes involved in financing packages to facilitate the completion of a deal.

In light of the rapidly ageing population and life expectancy, pension funds have a great potential. In 20 years from now, the population of over 65s should more than double, increasing from 11% to 25% of the total population. The ratio of active to non-active people should fall from 7 to 4. In addition, the retirement age is now 50 for workers, 55 for women and 60 for men. On this basis, pension fund assets should increase four times from Rmb 7400 billion ($1200 billion) up to Rmb 28,000 billion ($4000 billion) in 2020.

On top of life insurance, non-life insurance has great potential, especially car insurance. In 2012 the Chinese car market overtook the USA with an annual production of 20 million vehicles. The Chinese car market coverage does not exceed 3% as opposed to 95% in the USA. As institutional investors, Chinese insurance companies should be increasingly contributing to both the size and liquidity of financial markets.

Private Equity Funds

Even though private equity funds play a relatively marginal role in the Chinese financial markets, they are symbolic of the pragmatic approach of

Chinese leaders in charge of economic affairs. Private equity funds are the epitome of the wild, blood sucking, Western type of capitalism. However, the government has acknowledged the key role of private equity funds in financing high-tech start-ups and the nascent rapidly growing local firms.

As with most of the other equity funds, lack of "exit" is the major obstacle to the development of Chinese equity funds. In order to make a capital gain and rebuild their investment capacity, equity funds have to sell their participation, either by listing the company on a dedicated stock market such as the NASDAQ, or by selling to a larger group involved in this kind of business or to an investment company expecting to resell the stake with a capital gain.

Initially, Chinese equity funds were forced to sell their participation to off-shore markets or companies. Created in 1993, Aramco (Asian Strategic Investment Company) took a participation in many TVEs, small companies launched by local authorities to meet the needs of rural markets. In order to resell its participation, Aramco was forced to form off-shore investment companies listed on foreign exchange markets. In 1997, CICC (China International Capital Corp.), an investment bank affiliated to the State owned bank CCB (China Construction Bank), took a stake in a Chinese tile manufacturer, Eagle Brand Holding, which it managed to list on the Singapore Stock Exchange in 1999. Sohu.com, an internet company launched in 1996 and listed on NASDAQ, and AsiaInfo, a Chinese manufacturer of integrated management systems and a supplier of companies such as China Telecom, China Mobile, China Unicom and China Netcom, created a private equity fund which was finally listed on NASDAQ. In 1998 the Californian company Sinaset.com, and a computer program manufacturer got together to form SINA.com. Once again shareholders were forced to use an off-shore company listed on a foreign exchange market to sell the Chinese company. However, the opening of the Chinext market on the Shenzen Stock Exchange in 1991 and the development of Chinese investment banks improved the exit problem. The exit rate rose from 25% in 1997 to 47% in 2000 (the internet bubble), then it fell to 20% and has settled down at around 30% since then. From 1997 to 2012, the average exit rate was 29%, hardly lower than the US rate (34%).

Since then the market has been growing and diversifying. Chinese equity funds invested in high-tech firms (Shanda, Baidu, Focus) and in small, fast-growing companies (Mengniu, Li Ning, Yurun, Bohai Industrial Fund). Foreign investors such as investment banks (Warburg, Morgan Stanley), equity funds (Carlyle, Blackstone), and sovereign funds (GIC and Temasek in Singapore), created joint ventures with Chinese investors (SAIF, IDG, Ceyuan, Sequoia, Capital Today, TDF) (Table 8.6).

A great number of Chinese private equity funds have been formed on the initiative of local governments in partnership with foreign investment funds to provide financial backing to local small and fast-growing companies and to attract new ventures. Most of them have been initiated by government institutions. In 2011 the city of Beijing (Beijing Municipal Government) launched two equity funds with Blackstone and Carlyle, to take participations in local, fast-growing companies. In 2011 CDB (China Development Bank) formed a joint venture with the Asiatic fund MP Pacific Harbor Capital and the US fund Matline Paterson to create an equity fund focusing on Asian small and medium-sized companies. But foreign and privately owned companies were also involved. In 2011 the British insurance company, Prudential Financial, invested $500 million in a Chinese private equity fund dedicated to luxury goods and managed by Fosun, a diversified "private" group (pharmaceutical, mining, metal, real estate, entertainment), the owner of Club Mediterranée.

Table 8.6 The ten largest dedicated funds in China ($billion)

Bohai Industrial Investment Fund	3.07	(2006) (Boci Private Equity)
Hopu USD master Fund I	2.5	(2008) (Hopu Investment Mger)
CDH China Fund III	1.63	(2007) (China Management Cy.)
Yunfeng Fund	1.53	(2012) (Yunfeng Capital)
CDH China Fung IV	1.45	(2010)
Blue Ridge China	1.45	(2008)
Honey Capital Fund IV	1.39	(2008)
Citic Mianyang Private Equity Fund	1.38	(2009)
Trophy Property Development	1	(2008) (Winnington Capital)
Raffles City China Fund	1	(2008) (CapitaLand)

Source: Preqin 2014

In 2011 Pacific Alliance,[11] a Hong Kong-based fund, raised $1.7 billion to invest in yuan denominated assets. Chinese pension funds were now allowed to participate in private equity funds. However NSSF, the nationwide government owned pension fund, was recently authorized to dedicate 10% ($75 million) of its assets to private equity.

Venture capital is indeed an alternative source of funds for small high-tech and fast-growing companies that have no access to bank credit. However, the share of Chinese equity funds in the financing of Chinese companies remains marginal. The total funds collected by the equity funds (venture capital) did not exceed $100 million, i.e. 0.27% of GDP, as opposed to 0.61% in India, 1.06% in the UK and 1.42% in the USA.

Brokerage Firms

Chinese brokerage firms, most of them affiliated to an investment bank, are often suspected of misconduct. In August 2012, a mistake by a trader from the Chinese broker Knight Capital Group, triggered wide and unexpected market fluctuations which cost the brokerage firm $440 million in losses. In August 2013 the market was closed following a mistake by the government owned Everbright Securities. Following a failure of the computerized arbitrage system, stock orders were massively injected into the clearing system. The daily volume of transactions jumped from Rmb 7.27 billion to Rmb 23.4 billion ($3.8 billion) and, within minutes, the Shanghai stock index climbed up 5.6%. Many listed stocks, including the chemical and oil State owned Sinopec (China Petroleum & Chemical Corp.), which moved beyond its authorized 10% fluctuation margin, were automatically withdrawn from the market.

For a long time Chinese brokers were dealing in an unregulated area. Often, brokerage firms used to mix up their customers' transactions and transactions on their own accounts. Most of them were involved in trading rather than dealing, which is a source of extra earning. Acting as market makers, brokers would be in a better position to serve their customers. Following public offerings, allocation of delivered securities

[11] The main shareholder is Shan Wei jian, a former TPG officer.

was arbitrary. Relying on trading fees, most Chinese brokers neglected the other sources of profit such as underwriting and asset management, which have no impact on the capital base.

Following several costly mismanagement problems in 2015, the brokerage industry had to be restructured. PBOC and CSRC struggled to keep control of the market. More sensitive to the risks involved, CSRC requested the closure of failing brokers. More sensitive to market mechanisms, PBOC was more accommodating. Eventually, it was CSRC's point of view that prevailed. The most ill-managed brokerage firms were closed, the weakest were merged and requested to be backed up by strong and reliable banks. In January 2011 the government opened the broker's capital to foreign banks up to a 20–30% stake. As the brokerage business is mostly a service company, the magnitude of its total shareholding value is not very costly. JP Morgan took a participation in First Capital Securities, and Morgan Stanley in Huaxin Securities. In 2012, UBS was authorized to take a 95.42% stake in Shanghai Pumin Futures Brokerage Co. for Rmb 90 million ($15 million). Usually the size of foreign stakes is in line with the needed expertise or the lack of capital funds (Table 8.7).

Other Chinese brokerage firms such as Guotai Jun'an, Haiton Securities and Orient Securities (the former defeasance company turned into an asset management company), have foreign investors among their shareholders.

Table 8.7 Foreign banks having a shareholding in Chinese security firms

JP Morgan Chase (Liaoning Securities)
Royal Bank of Scotland (Galaxy Futures)
Newedge Group (CITIC Newedge Futures)
Rothschild (Shonghai Fund Management)
REFCO (Jingyi Futures du groupe Galaxy)
Goldman Sachs (Gao Hua Securities)
Crédit Agricole (Xingcai)
UBS (Beijing Securities)

Following the wave of mergers, the brokerage market is now highly concentrated. The 10 largest brokerage firms had accumulated a 50% market share (43.46% in 2015). The largest brokerage firms are China Yinhe Securities (6.5% market share), Guotai Jun'an (6.15%) and Haitong Securities (4.64%).

Asset Management Companies

Most of the commercial banks, investment banks, insurance companies and brokerage firms created affiliated asset management companies which are the usual extension of their core business. As usual, asset management companies have been dealing in a legal vacuum until the government felt the need to regulate the asset management business. In 1997 the State Council issued a directive: "*Provisional Measures for Securities Investment Fund*" followed by a CSRC circular: "*Pilot Measures for Open Ended Securities Investment Fund Management*". In 2001 three asset management companies had obtained a licence: Hua An Fund Management Company, Nan Fang Fund Management Company and Huaxia Management Company, all of them affiliated to investment funds. As a

Table 8.8 The largest asset management companies (% market share)

		Domestic shareholders	Foreign shareholders
China AMC	9.2%	90%	10%
Harvest	613%	100%	
Southern	5.66%	70%	30%
Bosera	5.27%	100%	
GF	5.18%	100%	
E-Fund	6.66%	100%	
Hua'an	3.36%	100%	
Dacheng	3.08%	100%	
Yinhua	2.85%	100%	
Full Goal	2.83%	7%	28%

Source: CSRC annual report

step further, the asset management companies were instructed to find the backing of a bank's network to strengthen their capital base, as well as to sell shares and provide operational and management expertise.

The defeasance companies which had been created in the early 2000s to buy back the non-performing loans from the four State banks, had built up a business of their own on this expertise. Initially, Orient, Great Wall and Cinda used to allocate tranches of their asset portfolios through bidding procedures, then turned to offering their experience in dealing with problematic assets. Now they are full-fledged asset management companies. Some of them have applied for a banking licence in order to extend their business range. Also the NSSF (National Social Security Fund) turned into an asset management service producer: in 2015 NSSF took over the management of the pension fund of the province of Guangdong (Table 8.8).

Rating Agencies

In spite of the rating agencies' failure, which triggered the 2008 global financial crisis, they are indispensable to the smooth functioning of the stock and bond markets. Market participants need an unquestionable measuring apparatus, managed by independent firms, to set up a common price for financial assets and make risk assessments. Following a wave of scandals, some Chinese companies have raised doubts over the accuracy of their documentation. Several Chinese companies have been delisted from the New York Stock Exchange (real estate) or Toronto (Sino Forest) following warnings from whistleblowers such as Muddy Waters, an investment research company.

In order to prevent the Anglo-Saxon dominance of the "Big Three" leaders (Standard & Poor, Moody, Fitch), the Chinese government launched a State owned rating agency, Datong Global Credit Rating, which has now captured a 25% market share. The largest Chinese companies are now required to be audited by a Chinese rating agency. To be authorized to operate in Mainland China, the foreign audit firms have to take a minority stake in a joint venture with a Chinese audit firm. The Hong Kong Stock Exchange which has built up its growth in the

IPO (Initial Public Offering) market upon reliable and demanding documentation requirements may be penalized by this decision. In November 2014, Alibaba was finally listed on the New York Stock Exchange because HKSE documentation requirements were found too stringent. Alibaba's shareholders (among them Jack Ma) were not prepared to comply with the HKSE regulation that prohibits listed companies whose legal status disregards the "one share, one vote" principle.

By regulating financial markets and financial institutions, it seems that the Chinese government is always wavering between opening up and increasing controls, between consumer protection and government policies, between liberalization and intervention. One way or another, financial institutions—State banks, investment banks, insurance companies, sovereign funds—that play a key role in the sensitive mechanics of financial markets, remain under tight government control, whether direct or indirect. In accordance with the policy of opening up, markets have increasingly opened to foreign participants, but they are always kept on the sidelines to make sure that they cannot rise up to a lead position. Their market share is marginal and they are kept to a minority share. Their contribution is restricted to transfers of technology and expertise. In some cases, foreign shareholders are politely requested to sell off their shares in a successful venture, and to start from scratch all over again.

9

Under-developed Financial Markets

The Bond Market

In Western countries, government debt was the first security market. This is understandable in view of the fast-increasing burden of government military expenditure. Due to the lack of a debt market, governments were forced to give up and make peace when kings had exhausted their financial resources. In the seventeenth and the eighteenth centuries, shares of the "chartered companies", such as Vereenigde Oostindindische Companie (1602), British East India Company (1600) and Compagnie Française des Indes Orientales (1664), were traded on the local market. In the nineteenth century huge government bond issues were traded on behalf of defeated countries (France 1871, China 1895 and Russia 1905). Shares of transport companies (railway, turnpike canals and the Suez Canal) were traded on the nascent market and later on in the century so were the shares of petroleum, mining and steel companies. Until the stock and bond market was opened to most of the largest industrial and trading companies China followed the same path, but China achieved within a couple of years what Western countries did over centuries.

D. De Rambures, F. Escobar Duenas, *China's Financial System*,
DOI 10.1007/978-3-319-40451-6_9

The Government Bond Market

The government debt is well known, but overall government debt is far more difficult to estimate. On top of government debt *sensu stricto*, there are a number of institutions which are backed by an implicit State guarantee such as the political banks (CDB), State owned banks (SOB) and companies (SOE), government departments enjoying financial autonomy (Minister of Railway, and local government borrowing.

Amounting to Rmb 48,000 billion ($7400 billion) by the end of 2015, the Chinese bond market is the world's third largest behind the USA ($35,000 billion) and Japan ($11,000 billion). The Chinese bond market is growing fast at an annual 35% rate. In the aftermath of the 2008 crisis and the succession of the recovery plan which injected billions of dollars into the markets, the overall indebtedness of the Chinese economy doubled in the next few years, from 170% of GDP in 2008 to 240% in 2015. On the bond market were traded over 2000 companies as opposed to 200 in the far more mature Honk Kong market. However, the Chinese bond market accounts for only 9% of GDP (50% in the USA), which translates into great growth potential.

In a market economy, government debt has two goals: the funding of the government budget deficit and the implementation of monetary policy. However, these two goals are not necessarily consistent with each other, and sometimes may be conflicting. This is the reason why in Western countries, fiscal and monetary policies are managed by two separate and independent institutions—the government and the central banks—based on two different sources of legitimacy, democratic for the former one and bureaucratic legitimacy for the latter. Therefore the system demands close cooperation between the two institutions. In case of conflict, the two bodies may be outbidding each other. For instance, the central bank may be attempting to raise the interest rate to offset the growing budget deficit, which in turn increases the servicing of the debt, and so on.

Until recently government debt was kept at a very low level. In a totalitarian type of government, tax income is settled in accordance with government expenditure. The maximum tax collected is based on the overall fiscal capacity of the country. However, since the 2008 financial crisis, the successive recovery plans set up by the government led to an increasing budget deficit. In 2016, the budget deficit should amount to 3.8% of GDP. In accordance to the 13th Five-year Plan approved in March 2016 by the Parliament (People's Congress), the Prime Minister, Li Keqiang, stated that tax income should not increase and that additional expenditures, such as growth of public investment to stimulate a declining growth rate, should be provided through additional government indebtedness.

Government bonds fall into three categories:

- Treasury bonds issued by the Minister of Finance to fill the gap between government expenditure and government resources,
- short-term notes or financial bills issued by the central banks to counteract the impact of foreign exchange inflow,
- policy bonds issued by "political banks" and "development banks" such as CDB (China Development Bank) which are not allowed to take deposits and rely entirely on bond issues (Figs. 9.1 and 9.2).

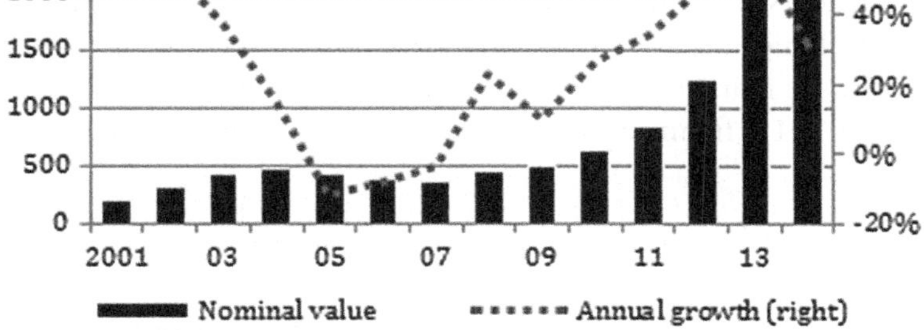

Fig. 9.1 The nominal value of exchange traded bonds
Source: China Securities Depository and Clearing Corporation

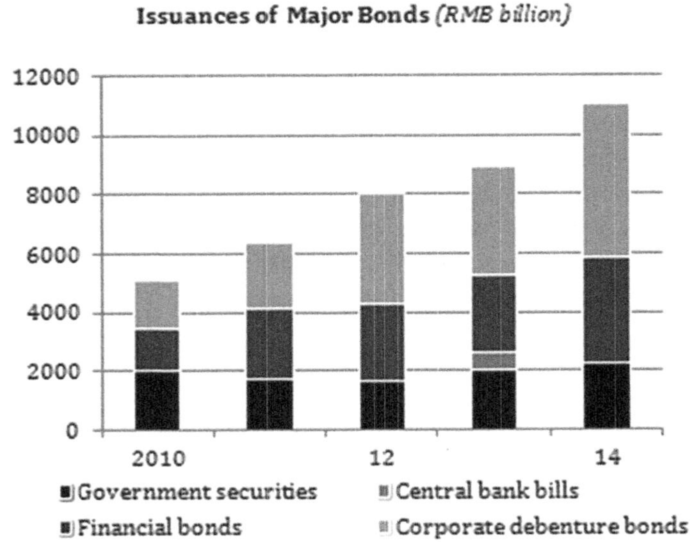

Fig. 9.2 Issuances of major bonds
Source: PBoC, NDRC, CSRC, CSDC

Since the 2008 crisis, Treasury bonds and government bonds shares have increased to fund the public investment needed to stimulate a decreasing growth rate as a follow up to the recovery plans. The policy bonds' share, mainly CDB (China Development Bank) bonds, kept increasing in line with the growing role of CDB in financing both domestic investments and foreign investment projects. Following the increasing foreign exchange outflow from early 2015, which sped up after the summer crisis, the market share of financial bills had drastically decreased. By the end of 2015, financial bills fell to 1.3% of government debt.

Government Borrowers

The main source of government debt is owed to other public borrowers who are backed by an implicit State guarantee: local government, State agencies, State owned banks and companies. Officially, local government debt is in the range of $2 billion, but according to some estimates local government debt accounts for $5000–10,000 billion, i.e. 75% of global government debt and 12.5% of GDP. Forced to resort to illegal sources of financing to meet the additional requirements from central government and unable to increase tax income, local governments turned to alternative sources of funds: the sale of government owned land, and borrowing from banks and bond markets. As land resources are getting exhausted, local governments turned to bank credit and ultimately to bond issues through affiliated borrowing platforms such as LGFVs (Local Government Financing Vehicles). Facing the fast-increasing indebtedness of local governments, the central government attempted to retake control of the local governments' indebtedness, like the Prime Minister Zhu Rong ji did in the 1990s.

In 2014, the central government authorized 10 provinces, mostly coastal provinces which are the least indebted (Zheijiang, Jiangsu, Shandong, Guangdong), to raise funds through bond issues. Such bonds are very attractive to Chinese investors, the interest rate being slightly over the government rate while the risk is meant to be the same. In 2015, central government instructed local governments to take advantage of the low interest rate to consolidate the debt by issuing long-term bonds to pay back short-term bank loans. The banks were instructed to subscribe to long-term bonds issued by local governments to get reimbursement for their short-term loans: a way to wipe out government loans from their assets and to increase their lending capacity. In 2015 the central government authorized 38 cities and provinces to borrow a total of Rmb 1 billion ($161 billion). The province of Jiangsu sold bonds of three, five, seven and 10 years' maturity at a rate ranging from 2.94% to 3.41%, slightly above government bond rates of the same maturity. As planned, 80% of the bonds were purchased by the banks. Local governments turned to the Hong Kong off-shore bond market (*dim sum* bonds)[1] opened to foreign investors to raise funds. In July 2014, Beijing Subway was the first public borrower to tap the *dim sum* market shortly after the issue of government bonds. Beijing Infrastructure sold a three-year Rmb 1.2 billion bond issue at a 3.75% interest rate, 115 bp (basis points or 1.15%) spread over the government bond issue, a rate substantially lower than the domestic rate charged to the same borrower (Table 9.1).

[1] So named after a local Hong Kong delicacy; wrongly translated by foreign investors.

Table 9.1 China's debt (%)

Central government	25.9% GDP
Local government	74.1% out of which
Provinces	18.9% out of which
Préfectures	22.7%
Districts	26.7%
Municipalities	5.9%

Source: CSRC annual report 2015

The total indebteness of the Ministry of Railways, a government agency heavily indebted through bank credit and bond issues, is said to have reached Rmb 1000 billion ($150 billion) or 5% of GDP.

Over the last few years, monetary policy is playing a growing role in overall economic regulation. On top of the usual instrument (interest rate, reserve requirement), the central bank's implementation of monetary policy is increasingly resorting to market instruments such as open market transactions which require wide, deep, liquid money and bond markets. More flexible, more targeted market interventions are aimed at regulating the money supply and fine tuning overall liquidity.

Placement Methods

Before market development, government bonds (and local government bonds) were sold through a quota system: the bonds issued were allocated to provinces, cities and banks according to a quota system set up by the government. Due to the lack of a well-organized secondary market, bonds were kept by the holders or repurchased by the banks until maturity. In the 1990s, government bonds were sold through a bidding system. As government bonds were included in the bank's reserve requirement and as they were tax free, but also because bank lending was limited to 75% of bank deposits, bank investment in government bonds was very attractive. More recently, government bond issues were performed through reverse bidding. Banks were bidding for a certain amount of bonds at a given price all over the maturity range. When the bond price is set by the central bank on the basis of the banks' bids, the volume of bonds of each maturity is allocated to the banks on a decreasing scale according to their bidding price and volume (Table 9.2).

Over 90% of the transactions took place on the interbank market which until recently was beyond the access of foreign banks and investors. Foreign investors had a marginal 2% market share. Following the 2015 crisis and in view of increasing market liquidity, foreign banks had been allowed to apply for access to the interbank market. However, foreign branches and affiliates had to be backed by the parent bank's guarantee, an extra cost, which makes foreign banks' bids uncompetitive. In addition, since the 2015 crisis, foreign investors were increasingly reluctant to get involved in yuan denominated assets. Also the turnover of government bonds on the secondary market was relatively low: 0.3–1.9% as opposed to 10% for the US Treasury Bonds and 5.9% for the Japanese Treasury Bonds.

The repo (repurchase agreement) market is more and more the main source of bank funding to settle banks' day-to-day cash management especially through short-term (a week) or very short-term (overnight) maturities. Since the 2013 cash run, banks are increasingly reluctant to lend to each other on the interbank market. Banks prefer to borrow from and lend to the central bank. On top of the compulsory reserve requirement and the volume of bank deposits with the central bank, banks keep the cash surplus on their central bank accounts, which is an obstacle to the efficiency of the central bank's monetary policy. If the central bank raises the bank's borrowing rate, banks are going to draw from their central bank account rather than increase their borrowing cost.

Table 9.2 Distribution of the bond market by investor (%)

Commercial banks	67.9%
Insurance companies	9.5%
Investment funds	7.1%
Individuals	1.1%
Other	14.4%

Source: CSRC annual report 2014

The Yield Curve

In theory, the interest rate charged to a bond issue should be established in accordance with the maturity of the bond and the credit worthiness of the borrower. In China the rate curve is distorted: interest rates are higher at the two ends of the curve (short- and long-term rates) and lower in between (medium-term rates). Generally speaking, the explicit or implicit State guarantee flattens the risk involved. Investors are convinced that whoever the actual borrower might be, the government will intervene to prevent risk spreading. The risk involved by the more or less direct State controlled borrowers and the subsequent rating are meant to be the same. Also, bond liquidity does not reflect the maturity but the demand side. Short-term Treasury bonds (under one year) are very attractive to a bank's cash management as government bonds are included in the bank's reserve requirement. Long-terms government bonds are very attractive to investors (insurance companies, development banks) in search of returns and long-term assets matching long-term liabilities, as government bonds are the only available long-term assets (Fig. 9.3).

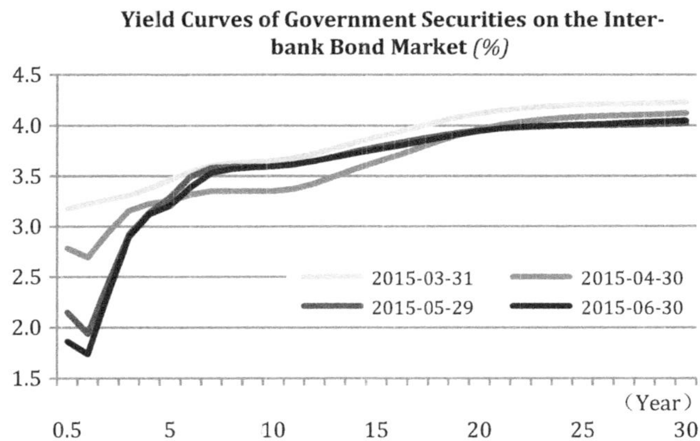

Fig. 9.3 Yield curves of government securities on the interbank bond market
Source: China Government Securities Trust and Clearing Co. Ltd.

The low inflation rate and the fall of foreign exchange reserves following the 2005 foreign exchange and stock crisis has dried up the volume of financial bills issued. As a result of its growing market share and liquidity, CDB's bonds are increasingly traded and used as a benchmark for other bond issues. The maturity range of government bonds has been lengthening again and again. In 1996 China placed a bond issue on the 100-year Yankee Bond market.

The Opening of the Bond Market

Within the framework of the policy of yuan internationalization, the government managed to widen access to the bond market for foreign investors and borrowers. In 2012, following Malaysia and Thailand's central banks' initiatives, the central bank of Japan issued a $10 billion 10-year bond issue on the Chinese market. In November 2015, the IMF decided to include the yuan among the special drawing rights (SDR; the IMF accounting currency) currencies (dollar, euro, yen and sterling) from 1 October 2016. Consequently, central banks have to increase their yuan denominated assets within their foreign exchange reserve, which should boost the government bond market. However, the impact should be marginal, as most central banks have already anticipated the move.

The Corporate Bond Market

As the Chinese government bond market was developing fast, the corporate bond market took off much later in the 2010s. As most potential borrowers were government owned companies financed by bank credits, financing through bond issue was useless. Following the 2008 crisis the government launched a huge $600 billion recovery plan. The banking sector was instructed to increase the volume of lending. As a result bank lending doubled in one year. The bulk of new bank loans was diverted to prestigious infrastructures, useless investments leading to over-capacities, and the purchase of securities. In the second half of 2009, as growth was recovering, the government was forced to rein in bank lending. Small companies turned to the informal credit market. Large companies, especially the State owned ones, turned to alternative sources of credit, i.e. the yet undeveloped corporate bond market. On the demand side, corporate bonds provided investors with a better return, rewarding a risk which was more or less the same as government risk. As the interest rates were lowered in the wake of the recovery plan, corporate bond prices increased.[2] Subsequently, the volume of corporate bond issues rose from Rmb 1500 billion ($150 billion) in 2010 to Rmb 4000 billion in 2014. Following the opening of Connect, a trading link between the Shanghai and Hong Kong stock exchanges, foreign investors (including Chinese holders of yuan balances in Hong Kong) disinvested to reinvest in domestic yuan bond issues providing a much better return. In 2015, following the summer crisis in the stock market which lasted over nine months, central banks lowered interest rates and reserve requirements in the expectation that this would halt the fall in stock prices. Hence, the market price of bonds sky rocketed.

As the market was developing, the spread between government bonds and corporate bonds narrowed, so that the interest charged to companies' bonds lowered along with borrowing costs. Before the 2015 stock market crisis, the average spread of corporate bonds above the 10-year government bonds was 1.92% in China as compared to 1.86% in India, 1.37% in Malaysia and 1.05% in North Korea. As growth of bank credits was slowing down due to the increased solvability ratio and more stringent lending criteria, the big State owned companies turned to the bond market as the spread between the three-year Treasury bonds and the interest charged to the corporate bonds fell from 3.7% in 2011 down to 1.3% in 2015.

The bond issuer should be large enough to tap the bond market. Therefore most corporate bond issuers are State owned banks and companies. In addition, currency denomination has been diversifying. In December 2015, CCB (China Construction Bank) managed to sell a Rmb 1 billion ($150 billion) bond issue, followed by $900 billion dollar denominated bonds issued by ABC (Agricultural Bank of China), and a three-year €500 million bond issue denominated in euro by Donfeng to finance the acquisition of European companies (such as the French car manufacturer Peugeot).

---

[2] Bond prices move in the opposite direction to interest rates. When the interest rate is decreasing, the bond price is increasing, and vice versa.

As most investors feel confident that in cases of default the government will intervene to bail out defaulting companies, investors are not really concerned about the issuer's risk. Cinda (China Cinda Asset Management Co.), an asset management company, was created in 2005 as a defeasance company to clean up the State bank's assets before being listed on the stock exchange. By definition Cinda assets are made up of bad loans, yet Cinda was listed on the Hong Kong stock exchange through a $2.2 billion public offering in 2013, followed in 2014 by a $1 billion issue on the bond market, and in 2015 by another $2 billion, at a rate close to the government rate. Between the 2014 bond issue and the 2015 transaction, rates of the five- and 10-year tranches lowered from 4% to 3% and 5.625% to 4.3% respectively.

The implicit government guarantee could be questioned if and when the government is willing to give up a defaulting company. On 23 October 2015, the manufacturer of solar panels, Chaori Solar (Shanghai Chaori Solar Energy Science & Technology Co.) went bankrupt as it could not meet its reimbursement of bonds. It was the "ideal" company to go bankrupt and the market was expecting a payment default, but at the last moment the company was bailed out. According to the debt restructuring plan, China Great Wall Asset Management Corp., a former defeasance corporation turned into an asset management company, and the Shanghai Eternal Sunshine Investment Management Corp., an investment company, delivered a guarantee to the 6300 holders of Chaori Solar bonds. In October 2015, SinoSteel, a State owned steel manufacturer, an affiliate of the government holding SASAC (State Owned Assets Supervision & Administration Commission), could not meet a Rmb 2 billion bond payment due date. Again the market was expecting the company to go bankrupt as the steel market was collapsing and steel companies were known to be near bankruptcy. At the last moment, the bond maturity was postponed.

In addition, to calm down bondholders' concern, banks were required by the government to swap companies' bonds against stocks so that companies' indebtedness and bank assets are lowered (but the bank exposure deteriorates). In the end, the short-term bank credit was swapped against long-term bonds subscribed by the banks while the bonds were swapped against companies' shares. It looks like a mere accounting trick.

Off-Shore Bond Issues

When Deng Xioa ping launched the policy of reform and opening up in 1979 shortly after his return to the Politburo (1978), the issue of foreign currency loans led to a heated argument between reformists and conservatives among its leaders. Conservatives were concerned about China's dependence on foreign countries. Reformists put forward that China needed funds to implement the transition to a modern economy. Deng was supporting the idea of the reform through opening up. Finally, China borrowed $220 million soft loans from Japan. Today, China does not need foreign funds anymore, but the Chinese economy needs foreign technology and Chinese companies need diversified borrowing sources.

In 2015 off-shore loans amounted to $127 billion while the outstanding volume of off-shore loans reached $776 billion (Fig. 9.4).

In 2007 Chinese companies were allowed to tap into foreign markets either through bonds sold on the market or bank loans. As a result the

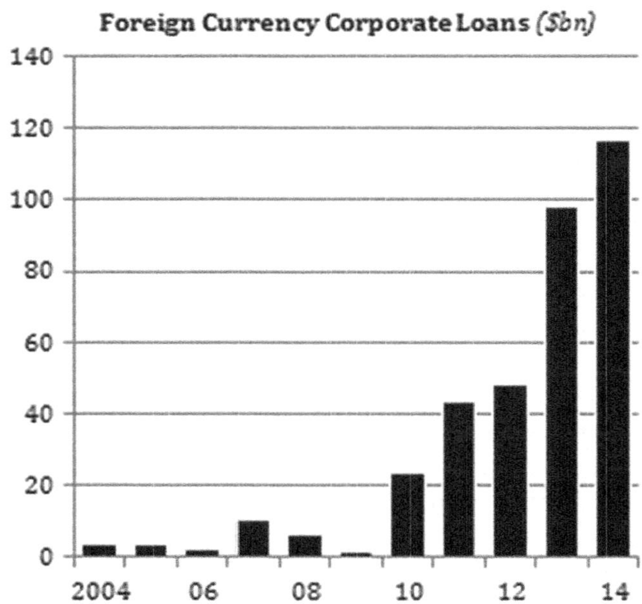

Fig. 9.4 Foreign currency corporate loans
Source: CBRC 2015

off-shore bond market took off in 2010 and has been growing fast since then. Off-shore bonds were very attractive for both issuers and subscribers. Until recently the interest rate of the borrowing currency (mostly US dollars and HK dollars) was lower than domestic rates while the borrowing currency was weakening against the yuan. For lenders the rate was higher than the domestic rate without the exchange risk since the bonds were denominated in US dollars. Chinese companies had access to an alternative source of borrowing in times of credit shrinkage.

Financing of Property Developers

Ever since the market started diversifying and extending transactions to the whole range of borrowing instruments the issues have been extended from State banks and State owned companies to commercial banks, private companies and property developers. Maturities were extended to both short-term and long-term bonds. Chinese banks were allowed to issue short-term (one to three years) CDs (Certificate of Deposit) while some issuers experienced longer-term bonds. In 2014, Aluminum Corp. of China and Yangzhou Coal Mining Co. issued two $700 million (each) perpetual bonds. Sino Ocean Land, a developer, sold perpetual bonds up to $400 million at a 10.25% coupon that is redeemable any time at the lender's request. Some Chinese companies have issued convertible bonds (*cocos*); bonds ranking behind ordinary bonds but before shares in case of default, which provide a better return than bonds, but at a lower risk than stocks. In 2015, China State Construction Engineering Corp., a State owned company, issued $238 million convertible bonds on the Hong Kong market.

Off-Shore Bond Market

The off-shore bond and loan market is of particular interest to Chinese developers and investors. In times of credit shrinkage at home, development and real estate companies turned to the off-shore market to raise the funds needed which were no longer available in Mainland China. Investors got a much better return than the rate offered by domestic borrowers, mostly State companies enjoying creditworthiness close to the government's one. Until recently, foreign currency off-shore borrowing proved to be very attractive: the interest rate was lower than the domestic borrowing cost and bonds/loans were denominated in a currency (US dollar) which was weakening steadily against the renminbi. The whole picture changed drastically after the 2015 foreign exchange crisis and the collapse of stock prices. US dollar rates increased while the yuan weakened against the US dollar. As the loans/bonds fell due, Chinese real estate companies had to reimburse loans/bonds denominated in a strengthening currency. However a default is no longer ruled out and it may well be an occasion for the government to remind investors of the moral hazard associated with Chinese bond issuers. In May 2015 (i.e. before the foreign exchange and stock market crisis), Kaisa (Kaisa Group Holding), a Shenzen-based property company, defaulted on US dollar bonds. Eventually Kwok Group, a family property group headed by Kwok Ying shing, acquired the Kaisa Group along with its liabilities. However, property developers kept tapping into the off-shore bond market. Late in 2015 (i.e. after the crisis), Greentown, a property group (Greenwood China Holding Ltd) based in Zheijiang (north of Shanghai), placed a five-year $1.4 billion bond issue at a 8.75–9% rate through an off-shore affiliate. However, if the issuing spree goes on, it is likely that the market will demand a higher rate to offset the growing risk, both the deteriorating sovereign bond (of China) and company (real estate) risk.

The *dim sum* bond market, foreign currency (mostly US dollar and HK dollar) bonds placed on a foreign market (mostly Hong Kong), has been growing fast since the first bond issuance. In July 2007, CDB (China Development Bank) sold a US dollar denominated bond on the Hong Kong market. CDB is a State owned "policy" bank and a large bond issuer that is priced nearly at par with government bonds. As expected the issue was a great success. Since then the off-shore bond market has been extended to other financial centres: in 2012 CCB (China Construction Bank) was the first Chinese bank to place a bond issue on the London market.

The *dim sum* bond market has been growing fast from 2010 to the extent that *dim sum* bonds met both issuers' and investors' needs. From an issuer's point of view, the *dim sum* bond market provided alternative sources of borrowing in times of credit shrinkage in mainland China. Hit by fast decreasing rates at home, foreign investors turned to more profitable investment opportunities. It soon appeared that both issuers and investors were mostly mainland Chinese companies. Chinese companies, authorized to keep all or part of their foreign income abroad, were looking for more rewarding bank balances. On the other side, most bond issuers were mainland Chinese companies or local affiliates.

The *panda* bond market (bonds issued by Chinese companies on an off-shore market, mostly Hong Kong, and denominated in yuan) is very attractive to both issuers and investors. For Chinese borrowers, *panda* bonds provide riskless liabilities since the bonds are denominated in renminbi, and are an alternative source of funds, as the bonds are placed on off-shore markets along with foreign investors' capital. For years *panda* bonds provided both a better return and an alternative investment for foreign investors. In addition, foreign companies exporting to China and getting paid in yuan were looking for investments denominated in yuan to match their yuan deposits. Until recently, the yuan income of foreign companies was not allowed to be swapped against another currency and had to be kept in yuan until it could be sold to another foreign company in search of yuan lending to match its foreign investment needs in China.

The first issuers of *panda* bonds were international finance organizations. In 2005 the IFC (International Finance Company), a World Bank affiliate, sold a Rmb 1.13 billion bond issue at a 3.4% rate. In 2013 the ADB (Asian Development Bank) placed a 10-year Rmb 1 billion bond issue at a 3.34% rate. As it could not be converted into another currency, the proceeds of the bond issue had to be used in Chinese investments. A number of Western banks owning substantial interests in mainland China such as the British HSBC (Hong Kong and Shanghai Bank) and the Australian ANZ (Australian & New Zealand Bank), tapped into the *dim sum* bond market as a new source of borrowing in yuan to match their yuan assets. In 2015, Daimler was the first Western corporate issuer to place a yuan denominated bond issue on the domestic bond market.

Since then the *panda* bond market has been diversifying in both location and maturities. For a long time the bond market was based in Hong Kong, which is under Chinese government control. More recently the yuan bond market has been extended to foreign financial centres. The central bank PBOC put together a number of swap credit lines with foreign central banks, and to start with the Bank of England, to ensure the supply of yuan and liquidity of the newly formed bond market. In November 2015 PBOC place a three-year Rmb 30 billion bond issue on the London market. The issue was six times over-subscribed and the interest rate was pulled down from 3.3% to 3.1%.

The Stock Market

China's Stock Exchanges were officially launched in December 1990 (Shanghai) and January 1991 (Shenzen) while the Hong Kong Stock Exchange joined mainland exchanges in 1997 when the British colony was transferred to China at the end of the 150-year lease treaty. On top of financial asset markets are the commodity markets scattered all over the country, close to production sites. In terms of country, Chinese markets rank second ($3697 billion) far behind the USA ($18,868 billion), but ahead of Japan ($3681 billion) and the UK ($3019) (see market capitalisation in Table 9.3).

Out of the ten largest stock capitalization, four are Chinese: Petrochina, ICBC (Industrial & Commercial Bank of China), China Mobile, Sinopec, the next one being China Shenshua Energy (30th). All of them are State owned companies. The three largest IPOs (Initial Public Offerings) are Chinese: ICBC ($21 billion in 2006), Agricultural Bank of China ($22.1 in 2010) and Alibaba ($25 billion in November 2014).

Table 9.3 Market capitalization ($ billion)

NYSE (New York Stock Exchange)	19,223
NASDAQ	6831
LSE (London Stock Exchange)	6186
TSE (Tokyo Stock Exchange)	4485
Shanghai Stock Exchange (SSE)	3986
Hong Kong Stock Exchange (HKSE)	3325
Euronext	3321
SSE (Shenzen Stock Exchange)	2285

Source: CSRC 2016

In terms of IPOs, until 2009 the NYSE was on top of the list. In 2010, Shanghai and Hong Kong issued $73 billion IPOs twice as much as the NYSE and NASDAQ combined. In 2011, HKSE issued $30.9 billion in IPOs, slightly above the NYSE ($30.7 billion) until Chinese IPOs were suspended. In 2015, when the stock listing resumed, Hong Kong was back in front place with $34 billion in IPOs. Due to the IPO's suspension following the 2015 stock crisis, the waiting list is said to have risen to several hundred companies.

The overall capitalization, the number of listed companies and the volume of transactions of Chinese exchanges have been growing fast, but markets are still unsophisticated, poorly diversified and the market for products under-developed. On the Shanghai Stock Exchange are listed over 2500 companies, as opposed to 200 on the Hong Kong Stock Exchange. All of the industries are quoted with a concentration on banking and finance. Most of the listed companies are State owned. High volatility, a lack of transparency, low market liquidity, the weak internationalization of Chinese markets as well as the lack of hedging instruments make trading difficult for both issuers and investors.

High Market Volatility

In 2014 stock prices sky rocketed to 80% and dropped by 30% the next year. There is no or very little connection between companies' profit records and prospects, and stock prices. The subsequent price volatility is owed to a wide range of factors: savings over-supply, limited investment opportunities, market narrowness, and lack of market makers and institutional investors.

The Chinese saving rate is unusually high (53% GDP in 2015), including the household saving rate (37%), as compared to other emerging markets. In the long-term, this is owed to a secular experience of instability and widespread feelings of insecurity, and in the short-term, to the lack of saving instruments. The nineteenth and twentieth centuries are one of the worst times experienced by the Chinese people.

For years the only saving instruments at the disposal of Chinese savers were bank savings accounts and government Treasury bonds, both of them poorly rewarded (3% or close to the inflation rate). Following the ongoing policy of interest rate liberalization, banks had extended the range of investments to WMPs, synthetic investments including several tranches of loans, and the trust or investment companies buying bank loans. The next type of investment is property, and finally financial assets: stocks and bonds, life insurance contracts and investment fund shares. According to the current government policy, investors keep moving from one to the other in search of a better return. For example, savers shift from bank accounts and Treasury bonds to the new investment products—WMPs and trust shares. When the government wants to stimulate the construction industry, which is a strong driving force of the whole economy, it lowers the rate of property loans, and savers move their savings from bank products to the property sector. When it is concerned about a property bubble, the government raises the down payment level and the interest rate of property loans, and Chinese savers move their savings to the stock market. When the government is concerned about a stock bubble, it increases the interest charged to bank loans granted to stockholders, and Chinese savers switch back to bank saving instruments, and so on.

This perpetual motion is driven by the everlasting imbalance between savings and investments, a combination of a high saving rate on one side, and lack of investment opportunities on the other. As mentioned above, this is partly owed to structural factors, but also it seems to be a deliberate policy on the part of the government, inherited from Maoist times. In Mao's though, driven by Marxist tenet, the industrial revolution was funded by the surplus funds extracted from the agricultural sector. All of the available savings were transferred from the agricultural sector to the manufacturing field. Later, in the early times the policy of reform and opening up, household savings were pulled from the consumption market to provide manufacturing capital investment. Today the government is attempting to redirect savings from investment in the manufacturing sector to the consumption one, as well as to the service industry and the innovation field.

Finally, the market imbalance is caused by the lack of market makers, institutional investors and hedging instruments. In Western countries, once the stock is listed and traded, a group of investment banks are in charge of looking after price stability. The market makers are bound to make a price, both ways (buyer and seller) to traders. In times of hectic market conditions, market makers are stabilizing agents. In addition, institutional investors (insurance companies, investment banks, investment funds, pension funds, equity funds and sovereign funds) are usually acting in order to cool down the market price and to absorb market fluctuations. But, on the Chinese stock market, the market share of institutional investors is in the range of 50% as compared to 80% in developed countries. Most Chinese institutional investors are State owned and tightly controlled by the government, which is both a strength and a weakness. As evidenced in the 2015 stock crisis, thanks to their powerful striking force, institutional investors may reverse market trends. But they are also waiting upon government instructions until market forces are too strong to be brought back under control. With the objective of stabilizing the market, government interference may deepen the crisis (Fig. 9.5).

However the use of indexes such as Shanghai SSI Composite index and MSCI (Morgan Stanley Commodity Index) led to the development of ETFs (Exchange Traded Funds) or trackers which reflect the markets' stability and return. The sharp growth of such hedging instruments since 2010 may have a flattening effect on market fluctuations.

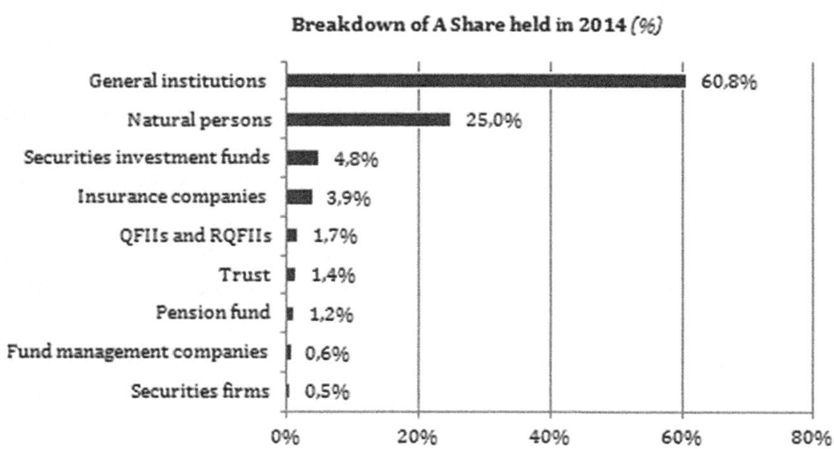

Fig. 9.5 Breakdown of A shares held in 2014
Source: CSRC

Market Integration

Trading business requires moving quickly and easily from one market to the next. Traders make profits out of small and brief spreads between two connected markets. For instance, as every spot transaction is made up of a cash leg and a security leg, the spread between the money market and the foreign exchange market on one side, and the stock market on the other, may produce a momentary profit opportunity under the condition that the markets are well connected.

In the early 1990s DVP (Delivery versus Payment) market infrastructures have been building up. Since then, processing facilities have been improved to lower transaction costs, facilitate operating processes and ensure market security and soundness. Today the overall cost of stock listing on the Shanghai Stock Exchange is in the range of 1% of the whole amount, as compared to 3% in Frankfurt and Tokyo, 4.5% in London and 5% in New York.

However, the market is still split and fragmented between different types of shares and market specializations. There are so-called A shares, H shares and Blue Chips which are quoted on a different market at a different price and are not fully convertible. A shares are shares denominated in yuan and traded on mainland Chinese markets, i.e. the Shanghai and Shenzen stock exchanges. H shares are shares denominated in foreign currencies (and off-shore yuan) traded on the Hong Kong stock exchange. Blue Chips are Chinese companies' shares, mostly State owned companies' shares listed on foreign exchanges (mainly American, i.e. the New York Stock Exchange and NASDAQ). Moreover, A shares are not fully convertible: only one-third of the issued A shares are negotiable, two-thirds being frozen. Also, the volume of the float, i.e. the number of listed and traded shares as a percentage of the whole amount, is relatively small, as low as 5%, as compared to the Western market where the float is usually no less than 30%. In addition, stock issues are often conditional on a "lock up" clause according to which the main shareholders are not permitted to sell the new shares during a given period of time, from a minimum of six months up to 3–5 years.

On top of the shares' fragmentation, Chinese stock markets are fragmented as well. Initially, the three Chinese exchange markets, i.e. Shanghai, Shenzen and Hong Kong, were highly specialized. On the Shanghai market big State owned companies' shares and government bonds were traded; on the Shenzen market, high-tech and small companies' shares following the creation of ChiNext in 2009 were traded; in Hong Kong, the largest companies were opened to international investors. Since then, the Shanghai market has extended the range of securities traded and the market has been extended to government bonds, commodities and futures markets. The largest Chinese companies, State owned companies, used to be listed at the same time on the Shanghai and the Hong Kong markets. In order to back the domestic markets, most of the shares of the largest companies had been repatriated from New York (Petrofina) and Hong Kong back to Shanghai. The trading of government bonds is split between Beijing and Shanghai. Now the Shanghai Stock Exchange is increasingly competing with the Hong Kong Stock Exchange on the whole range of financial assets, including foreign denominated corporate bonds and stock issues. As the information requirement and the listing conditions of the Hong Kong Stock Exchange are more demanding than Shanghai's, some companies are inclined to seek listing on the Shanghai market rather than the Hong Kong one. The number of companies listed on the Shanghai Stock Exchange is 10 times greater than that of Hong Kong.

As the same shares are traded on both on-shore and off-shore markets, foreign exchange rates may produce significant spreads between shares traded on different markets. The central bank is forced to intervene in the foreign exchange market to lower the spreads between on-shore and off-shore rates, and keep exchange rates and stock prices in line.

The Hong Kong Stock Exchange

In the early 2000s the Hong Kong market took advantage of the "privatization" era. It was customary to list an affiliate bank or company on the Hong Kong Stock Exchange (e.g. CITIC Pacific) when listing a parent company. Usually, the largest State owned companies were listed on both the Shanghai and the Hong Kong markets, the former dedicated to Chinese investors while the latter served international investors. The 10 largest companies listed on the Hong Kong Stock Exchange are State owned companies. Like the Shanghai market, the Hong Kong market concentrates on banking, finance and real estate (Wanda, Vanke). More recently, the Hong Market benefited from a new listing wave of regional banks. In 2016 the China Zheijiang Bank (Zheijiang is a province south of Shanghai) was listed through a $1.67–1.75 billion IPO along with some other regional banks such as the Bank of Tianjin ($1.2 billion), Qingdao Bank, Jinzhou Bank and Zhengzhou Bank, all of them located in the south-east coastal provinces.

Since 2011, the Hong Kong Stock Exchange is managed by a private company, HKE (Hong Kong Securities Exchange and Clearing Ltd). The market is regulated by a supervision agency HKSFC (Hong Kong Securities and Futures Commission). Founded in 1857 and managed by the British for 150 years, the Hong Kong Stock Exchange has a great reputation. The information requirements and the listing criteria are stringent. In 2010 HKSFC withdrew a textile company, Harnegy Thin Film Power Group, from the market after the Hanergy stock price fell by 47% within minutes, wiping out $3 billion in losses at once.

However, such a set of demanding standards may be counterproductive. Since a major scandal took place in the 1920s, the Hong Kong Stock Exchange does not authorize the listing of companies that do not stick to the "one share, one vote" principle. This requirement is an obstacle to the listing of high-tech and fast-growing internet companies such as Alibaba, Tencent and Baidu. The founding shareholders want to have a double voting right to keep control of the company in spite of the successive capital increases needed to back the fast growth. In 2014, for this reason, Alibaba's IPO shifted to the New York Stock Exchange. Given that 75% of broker fee income is owed to IPOs, the Hong Kong Stock Exchange may be forced to soften its listing criteria.

In 2012, HKSFC, the world's largest commodity market, acquired LME (London Metal Exchange), created in 1877, for $2.2 billion. Asian countries account for half the world's metal consumption. This business extension to commodity markets is a sign of a successful diversification process to keep competing with the Shanghai market.

Stock Connect

On Monday 17 November 2015 Stock Connect started operating, a direct link between the Shanghai Stock Exchange and the Hong Kong Stock Exchange. By using the Stock Connect canal, Shanghai investors had access to securities traded on the Hong Kong market. Hong Kong investors, including foreign investors, had access to securities traded on the Shanghai Stock Exchange. The main aim of Stock Connect is to give foreign investors the opportunity to buy and sell securities on the Chinese domestic market while bypassing the lengthy registration procedure to get a QFII (Qualified Foreign Institutional Investor) licence, which allows them to buy and sell Chinese securities within certain limits (see Chap. 10). The volume of transactions is obviously capped within limits. In the north-south canal (Shanghai-Hong Kong), the maximum volume of daily transactions is $10 billion a day and a maximum outstanding position is $300 billion. In the south-north canal (Hong Kong-Shanghai) the maximum volume of daily transactions is $3.5 billion and the maximum outstanding position is $250 billion.

So far the Connect system did not prove to be as successful as expected and the ceiling was far from being reached. After some operational problems, foreign investors had been discouraged by regulations. On the opening day, the tax treatment of capital gains was still unknown. Stock Connect is reserved to institutional investors. The users must hold a minimum $500,000 deposit to access the Connect system, which exempts most individual investors. Securities must be delivered before they are sold, which bans institutional investors and fund managers from the market since they cannot take advantage of short fluctuations and price spreads between the two markets. Following the opening of the Stock Connect direct link, the link to fill the gap between the two markets did not work: before Stock Connect was operating, the A shares (Shanghai) and the H shares (Hong Kong) of the same companies were at par; more than one year after, the H shares had an average 30% premium against the A shares. Last but not least, foreign investors are reluctant to get involved since the stock market 2015 crisis. Until they have a better market visibility, most of them are in a wait and see position. In 2016 Stock Connect was extended to Shenzen.

The Lack of Transparency

In theory, in a well regulated market, all users should have access to the same information. Transparency is indispensable to effective market mechanisms. But transparency is not viewed as a major feature of China's highly centralized and secretive regime. Markets are biased by insider trading, price rigging, false information and missing data.

Placement Methods

According to the CSRC regulations, the listing of a company is subject to a certain number of rules: the company should have a minimum equity of Rmb 50 million, 1000 shareholders owning 1000 shares each and profit records over the past three years. No shareholder should own more than 5% of capital shares. The core group of shareholders must hold new shares for a minimum of six months.

Although the 2014 regulations provide that the CSRC's role is limited to checking that legal conditions are fulfilled, in effect CSRC gets into the details of transactions: date of issuance, amount, issuing price, percentage of the float, leading banks, underwriters, allocation of shares issued between the different stock markets in case of simultaneous issuance on the Shanghai and Hong Kong markets, allocation of shares in case of over-subscription, etc.

More often than not, CSRC set up the issuing price at the bottom end of the bracket, while the number of shares sold was purposely limited to ensure a successful issuing. As a result the stock price used to jump in the first trading day and the following days, until the stock price fell after the initial spree was over as it was not supported by a group of market makers, i.e. institutional investors selected to back the market by meeting the traders' transactions. In most cases, before the public placement takes place, a capital increase is made through a private placement among institutional investors selected by the CSRC, to make sure that the capital increase is under control.

Information Weaknesses

Chinese companies have a bad reputation as far as the supply of accurate information is concerned. The Hong Kong Stock Exchange is praised for its demanding listing criteria. In 2012 the Chinese company Renren,[3] an internet social network, and its bankers were accused of deliberately misinforming investors as the company was about to get listed on NASDAQ. Lacking reliable track records, an internet company is valued on the basis of the number of users. According to the placement prospectus, the number of steady users was 131 million until the market learned that 31 million used the network less than once a month. Even though Renren was still making losses, the company raised $740 million in May 2011, which valued the loss-making company at 65% of the total sales.[4]

One of the favourite tricks of Chinese real estate companies seeking to get listed on the NYSE is the so-called "reverse merger". A loss-making Chinese company buys a small listed company, removes the loss-making assets to the parent company, transfers profitable assets to the listed company, changes the name and makes a capital increase. In 2012 two Chinese businessmen, Ming Zhao and Li Ping, managed to extract $115 million from American investors through an "empty shell", Puda Coal Inc., traded on the NYSE until it was noticed that the only shareholder of Puda Coal was the Chinese coal mining company, Shanxi Coal. Ming Zhao had taken over Shanxi Coal, a loss-making mining company on the brink of bankruptcy, sold 49% of Shanxi Coal shares to Citic Trust, an equity fund affiliated to CITIC (a State owned investment bank) and listed Shanxi Coal on the NYSE in 2005 through a "reverse merger" with

[3] Like "renminbi" (the People's money), "*ren*" means a man, the people and the virtue of humanness.

[4] As a matter of comparison, at the same time (January 2011), Facebook was valued $50 billion, i.e. 25 times the total sales.

Puda Coal. Finally, Chinese shareholders made a capital increase in the American affiliate after transferring loss-making assets from the affiliate company to the parent company, and profit-making assets from the parent company to the American affiliate.

Since 2009, several Chinese companies (such as Sino-Forest, Cleantech Innovation) have been delisted from North American stock exchanges, while several others (such as Harbin Electric, Orient Paper and Bodisen Biotech) are under scrutiny. In 2011 Deloitte Touche Tohmatsu LLP, the audit company selected by Longtop, a Chinese software company listed on the New York Stock Exchange, resigned as it refused to endorse the company's accounts.

Since 2009 the HKSFC, the Hong Kong market regulation agency, is no longer in charge of supervising the audit firms. The Hong Kong Stock Exchange is now forced to accept the authorized Chinese audit firms. In 2011 Tsingtao, the well-known beer manufacturer listed on the Hong Kong Stock Exchange since 1993, gave up its Hong Kong audit firm PwC (PricewaterhouseCoopers) and Western accounting standards, to shift to the mainland PwC Zhong Tian LLP, one of the 12 Chinese audit firms which had been granted an audit license. As 66 of the 163 Chinese companies listed on the Hong Kong Stock Exchange are also traded on the Shanghai Stock Exchange, it is likely that a number of Chinese companies will move to the less demanding Chinese audit firms.

The Internationalization of China's Stock

The internationalization of Chinese stock markets worked both ways, in and out: foreign investors were authorized, under certain limits, to buy Chinese domestic securities, and Chinese investors were allowed to buy foreign securities on an experimental basis.

Since 2003 the CSRC (China Securities Regulatory Commission) has granted QFII (Qualified Foreign Institutional Investors) and DQFII licences (Domestic Qualified Institutional Investors) to foreign banks and institutional investors. But the opening is tightly controlled. The QFII licences are granted to foreign banks, including overseas affiliates of Chinese banks (most of them located in Hong Kong), while RQFII licences are granted to foreign institutions holding yuan balances used to purchase domestic securities. However, the QFII scheme is still marginal: by the end of 2014, the volume of stocks purchased within the QFII scheme did not exceed 0.4% of the overall Chinese stocks. Today (2016) 152 foreign banks have been granted QFII licences. Each QFII licence is limited to a certain amount and the overall QFII licence should not exceed a global ceiling, which is obviously lower than the total amount of QFII licences. The global QFII ceiling has been steadily lifted from $20 billion (2003) to $80 billion (2012), and then from $80 billion to $150 billion (2013). In 2013, CSRC granted an extra $910 billion QFII licences to 11 non-banking foreign institutions.

On the other side, the opening of foreign markets to Chinese investors is far more limited. A pilot experiment is in process in Wengzhou, where Chinese investors are allowed to buy foreign securities on overseas markets. If the experiment proves to be successful, it might be extended to the whole market, under some limits of course.

The opening of the domestic bond market took place much later. In May 2015, 32 foreign banks (including HSBC and Morgan Stanley) were authorized to buy domestic bonds. Amounting to $6.5 billion (2016), the Chinese bond market is the third largest in the world, behind the USA and Japan. According to PBOC (2016), Rmb 713 billion ($115 billion) yuan denominated domestic bonds are owned by foreign investment funds, i.e. more than the Rmb 601 billion ($95 billion) owned by Chinese investment funds. In September 2014, CSRC authorized the Hong Kong affiliates of two "foreign" banks, one foreign and one Chinese, HSBC (Hongkong and Shanghai Banking Corporation) and BOC (Bank of China), to place renminbi denominated bond issues of Rmb 1 billion ($157 million) and Rmb 10 billion ($1.570 billion) on the domestic market (panda bonds).

In 2015, the Chinese government was induced to widen access to the domestic market for foreign investors to stimulate demand for falling domestic securities. However, following the combined stock crisis and foreign exchange crisis, the collapse of Chinese stock and weakening yuan, foreign investors were reluctant to buy Chinese yuan denominated stocks. Instead, most of them were selling their yuan assets.

The 2015 Stock Crisis

On Friday 26 June 2015, the Chinese stock market lost over 7% within one day. Over the next two weeks, Shanghai SCI 300, the Shanghai Stock market index, was falling by 30%, from 5166 (12 June 2015) down to 3687 (3 July 2015). The crisis wiped out Rmb 18.7 billion ($3 billion) worth of stock capitalization. After several days, the PBOC governor, Zho Xiu chuan, made a statement that the move was transitory and everything was under control. The crisis was going to be "a good lesson" to the hateful "speculators", those who were short selling the yuan. But the stock crisis kept deepening.

In the Zhongnanhai complex, the site where all the Party leaders and their families live, close to the Forbidden City, meetings followed meetings. The "reformists" led by Zhu Xiao chuan, Chairman of the central banks, were supporting market mechanisms. Sooner or later the market would react and bounce back. The "conservatives" led by Li Jou wei, Minister of Finance, were worried about the likely impact on economic and social stability. They took this opportunity to strengthen State control. As usual in times of crisis, the State Council was leaning towards political and social stability priorities. Consequently reforms were postponed while the central bank and the CSRC were instructed to calm down the markets. But it was too late: the market engine was working full speed and foreign media followed suit.

In the first stage, PBOC took a set of usual measures: decreased interest rates, decreased reserve requirements, and decreased compulsory bank deposits with the central bank, which led to an injection of Rmb 470 billion ($70 billion) of fresh liquidity into the market with the expectation that the banks would take advantage of additional money to increase loans to investors.

However, the crisis kept deepening and the stock market's collapse went on. The central bank shifted to less orthodox measures. Shortly after forbidding bank loans to buy stocks, PBOC made a 180-degree turn and gave instructions to banks and brokers to increase their lending. The 21 largest brokerage firms were requested to transfer 15% of their assets ($42 billion) to a government owned brokerage firm CSF

(China Securities Fund Corp.) in charge of buying securities to hold up stock prices. CSF was lending to listed companies to buy back their own shares and allocated a Rmb 260 billion ($40 billion) lending facility to renew margin calls at maturity. A Rmb 120 billion ($19 billion) relief fund was launched by SAC (Securities Association of China). It was then forbidden for State holdings to sell State companies' shares, and for State companies to sell affiliates' shares for the next six months. IPOs on the stock markets were cancelled and postponed.[5] Some 95% of the listed stocks were withdrawn: of these 41% were withdrawn on the grounds that they had reached the 10% fluctuation limits within one day, so that only 93 stocks were traded out of the 2879 stocks listed.

As stock prices kept falling, the government resorted to far more stringent measures. The media were instructed to give only a "nice picture" of the stock markets. State companies' leaders were forbidden to sell company shares they owned. Legal proceedings were initiated against "malicious" stockholders, "speculators" who were short selling and spooning[6] Chinese stocks. They were prosecuted on the grounds of "insider trading": they had access to insider information and were able to "influence the prize formation mechanism". Then 26 brokerage firms were suspected of fraud and closed. Several traders from CITIC Securities and Guoten Securities, two government owned brokerage firms, were arrested. A journalist, Wang Xiao lu, a member of the well-known business magazine, *Caixin*, made a public confession on State TV, CCTV: he confessed to have dispatched information along with "subjective" comments of his own, likely to cause "panic and disorder". He was not prosecuted for dispatching false news, but for dispatching real news which may cause trouble.[7]

The fall of stock prices was stabilized in July–August 2015, and at that time of year markets were usually much less volatile, but the stock crisis resumed in September and sped up in early 2016. On Monday 4 January

[5] As a result the planed CICC capital increase was postponed so that KKR and TPG Management 10% stakes were frozen.

[6] Simultaneous stock purchase and sale to take advantage of short-term fluctuations.

[7] "I should not publish news which had a major negative impact on the markets, at such a sensitive time ... I regret and I am willing to confess my crimes.", originally reported in The *People's Daily*, 2015.

2016, the SCI 300 index (Shanghai Composite Index) fell by 7% within one day, and SCI (Shenzen Composite Index) fell by 8.2%. The next day, PBOC injected $20 billion into the market within one day. Alibaba's stock price fell below the issuing price. In December 2015, CSRC set up circuit breakers to take effect on 1 February 2016. If a stock price loses 5%, it is withdrawn for a while; if a stock price falls by 20%, it is withdrawn for a three-month period. As stock prices kept falling, margins were narrowed, from 10% to 7%, and the suspension time was lengthened from three to five months. The circuit breakers were re-established and finally removed for good. Rather than lowering stock fluctuation, the circuit breakers dispatched a wrong signal to the market and sped up stock price falls.

Such a hectic policy caused dreadful consequences. The government's credibility was at stake and stock volatility had increased. The number of securities accounts fell from 75 million in June 2015 to 51 million one month later. China's stock market crisis was spreading to foreign markets, first to south-east Asia, then to the whole world. Foreign investors were unable to understand these erratic measures. They stayed aside waiting for better market visibility, or they required a discount to resume buying Chinese stocks. A number of Chinese savers had lost substantial amounts which may have lowered consumption (the wealth effect) at a time where the government was attempting to stimulate internal demand and household consumption. In the meantime, structural reforms were postponed.

Following the yuan devaluation and the stock's collapse, the Chinese government was at a crossroads: either it had to move to a fully convertible currency to stop foreign exchange outflow and to pursue the reform policy, or backpedal and re-establish foreign exchange controls on capital movements. In times of crisis, the Chinese government has always retreated.

The Chinese security markets are tightly controlled by the government through the PBOC and CSRC's close supervision and oversight. The Chinese government has undertaken a long-term policy of opening up the bond and stock markets. An increasing number of foreign investors have access to China's stock markets through the QFII and Connect systems. But the market share of foreign investors remains marginal, less than 1% of total stocks. In the light of the 2015 stock market crisis, government interference impedes market mechanisms from working properly, and this may be counterproductive. In June 2015's foreign exchange crisis, the market believed that the central bank was about to devalue the yuan while in reality it was actually struggling to keep the yuan exchange rate within the margin. In August 2015's stock crisis, late, erratic, disproportionate and untimely measures made the crisis worse. As soon as the crisis blew up, market reforms were suspended and postponed.

10

An International Non-Convertible Currency

Foreign exchange policy is an inherent part of the policy of reform and opening up promoted by Deng Xiao ping: opening up the economy is the reform's instrument. As the foreign exchange rate is set by the central bank, the Chinese government managed to neutralize foreign exchange policy and keep a tight control over fiscal and monetary policy. In addition, the growing volume of foreign exchange holdings was indispensable to overcome a difficult and dangerous transition period from a close planned economy to an open market economy. Now the government has undertaken a no less difficult and dangerous transition from a public investment-led economy to an economy driven by household consumption, the service industry and innovation.

Like the transition to a market economy, growing exposure to the outside world and the steady move to currency convertibility were aimed at improving companies' productivity and competitiveness. Like the market economy, the Chinese government was willing to open Chinese companies to overseas markets, provided that it kept control over the whole process. As usual, political and economic issues are tightly intermingled.

D. De Rambures, F. Escobar Duenas, *China's Financial System*,
DOI 10.1007/978-3-319-40451-6_10

China's leadership over South-East Asia demands integrated regional economies and markets. Integrated south-eastern markets require an increasing use of the yuan overseas. Is a non-convertible currency suited to becoming an international currency?

The Targets of China's Foreign Economic Policy

By order of priority, the aims of the overseas economic policy can be summarized as follows:

- to ensure access to raw materials badly needed by the fast-growing Chinese economy and the thirsty Chinese industry,
- to guarantee access to modern technologies, indispensable in moving from an investment-led economy to a service-propelled economy; meanwhile China's scientists and engineers have developed made in China innovative products and processes,
- to support direct foreign investments so that the Chinese economy is steadily integrated within the world's value chain,
- to create "national champions", Chinese companies able to compete with world leading supra-national companies,
- to promote Chinese leadership over South-East Asia,
- to back up Chinese international business.

The WTO Membership

Free access to foreign markets is indispensable to Chinese exporters, but more importantly to importers of raw materials needed by the fast-growing Chinese industry. China is not only the world's largest exporter ahead of Germany and Japan, but it is also the largest importer of oil, coal, copper, aluminum, steel, nickel, etc. China is often both the largest exporter and the largest importer of the same products. For example, China is by far the largest coal producer (over 50% of the world production) and consumer, but it is also the largest importer. China is the largest oil importer while it is the fourth largest producer behind the USA, Saudi Arabia and Russia.

Thanks to its highly centralized system, China is in a position to adjust both protectionist and free trade measures in response to a moving and diversified international environment. In order to prevent social disturbances, strikes and uprisings of unpaid and laid-off workers, the Chinese government managed to keep alive bankrupted companies in critical industrial sectors and State owned companies that used to guarantee the workers' "iron bowl of rice". The government kept alive loss-making steel companies to prevent huge lay-offs. For a while the government supported overseas dumping prices. When the European Union (the largest foreign steel market) threatened China, the Asian giant stepped back, closed unprofitable and dangerous coal and iron mines, increased inventories, and finally authorized the steel companies to lay off workers, triggering a wave of strikes and demonstrations by thousands of unemployed and unpaid workers.[1]

In such a context China's entry to the WTO (Word Trade Organization) in December 2001 was crucial to guarantee free access to developed markets and to sources of raw materials. However, China is more inclined to bilateral relations rather than multinational organizations which are often controlled by Western developed countries and more precisely by the USA. China built up a network of bilateral supply agreements, "infrastructure against raw material" agreements, with Latin American, African and Middle Eastern countries according to which China provided the construction of infrastructures (often the infrastructures needed to open up extracting sites) against the long-term supply of raw materials at market prices. In 2007, China tied up a bauxite supply agreement with Guinea against $3 billion infrastructures (far more than the annual GDP of the African country) in the back yard of the European Union. In 2011, China completed an oil supply agreement with Brazilian Petrobras against a $10 billion line of credit to Brazilian companies to finance imports of made in China equipment and capital goods. China is now Brazil's largest trade partner, right in the back yard of the USA.

[1] The Chinese PLA (People's Liberation Army) was instructed by the government to recruit laid-off workers, while on the other side the five-year military plan aimed at decreasing the number of soldiers and increasing technological weapons.

The centralized lending system of China that combines CDB soft loans, EXIM export and import loans, CIC shareholdings, State bank lending, and foreign direct investment of State owned companies, allowed China to grant *ad hoc* and competitive financing packages, granted on a case by case basis and suited to the needs of the developing and raw material producing countries. In 2015, China completed a $15 billion agreement with Argentina for the construction of two nuclear power plants,[2] 100% financed through a Chinese financing package.

Opening up to the world market is now needed more than ever as the Chinese economy is moving to a consumption led economy. Free trade is needed to import Western products that fit with the more and more Westernized consumption behaviour of modern-day Chinese consumers.

The South-East Asia Free Trade Area

In Chinese, China is *zhong guo*, i.e. "Middle Empire" (*zhong*: middle and *guo*: territory). China is the hub of the world and civilization. Although China is meant to be a multi-cultural country that includes 55 recognized minorities,[3] it is resting on Han nationalism. The Han people amount to 95% of China's population. For centuries China was a boundless mainland empire ruling over neighbouring barbarian tribes. Now China is a Westphalian type of nation, one among many others, within recognized frontiers.[4] In order to balance the USA's overwhelming influence on most of the after-war multinational organizations, China has joined regional multinational organizations such as APEC (Asia Pacific Economic Cooperation) on its east flank, and the Shanghai Club (Shanghai Cooperation Organization) on its west flank.

In 2013, in accordance with President Obama's "pivot" policy (shifting the emphasis from the Atlantic to the Pacific), the American

---

[2] The first nuclear power plant will be built using a Canadian process, and the second one using a Chinese one.

[3] China's flag is red (the communist as well as the energy symbolic colour) with a yellow star (the emperor's colour) on the upper staff side surrounded by four, smaller, yellow stars, i.e. the Han people surrounded by four minor people: Mongolian, Manchurian, Tibetan and Uighur.

[4] By definition an empire is limitless and has no legal borders: this is the reason why China is in dispute with all the border countries.

administration took a free trade zone initiated by Chile, Singapore and New Zealand, to build up an ocean wide free zone, the TPP (Trans Pacific Partnership), including all of the coastal countries. In 2014, on the occasion of the APEC annual meeting in Beijing, China put forward a proposal to build up a wide trading zone, FTAAP (Free Trade Area of Asia Pacific).

In September 2015, China scored the first point by launching the AIIB (Asia Infrastructure Investment Bank), a regional development bank with a $100 billion paid-up capital, half of it being supplied by China. Most of the closest US allies joined the new development bank, including the UK, Germany, France and South Korea (but not Japan) in spite of strong US pressures.[5] The next month, the USA scored the next point by announcing the creation of a new Free Trade Area: the TPP, including all of the countries bordering the Pacific Ocean. However, the TPP agreement is still far from being ratified by the US Congress as the Republicans, the unions and the President elect are all opposed to it.

Later on, President Xi Jing ping launched the very ambitious several billion worth "New Silk Road", "One belt, one road" programme. So far China's trade with the rest of the world had been mostly by sea. All of China's oil supply is channelled through the Malacca Straights. If an alternative land road existed, such as Marco Polo's "silk road" in the fifteenth century, the average transportation time could be shortened from one month to one week for non-heavy goods, which fits the modern just-in-time supply requirements. In addition, this huge transportation project would be beneficial to China's dynamic and highly competitive construction and public work firms.

The Shanghai Club SCO (Shanghai Cooperation Organization) was launched in 2010 by Russia. Initially, the SCO's aim was to curb spreading Islamic terrorism in central Asian countries: Kazakhstan, Uzbekistan, Turkmenistan, Tajikistan and all countries bordering China's province of Xing kiang. Under China's influence, the Shanghai Club turned into an economic, financial and trade organization focusing on raw material supply and swap agreements. China built a 4000-mile pipeline connecting Central Asia's oil and gas producing countries to the industrial

[5] The companies of the allied countries did not want to miss the bidding opportunities of AIIB financed construction and public work projects.

provinces of north-east China. Just as two centuries ago, in the good old times of the "Big Game", when the Powers (the UK, Russia and China) were struggling to get control over central Asia (Afghanistan was at the crossroad of India, China and Russia), Central Asia is again a battlefield where Big Powers are challenging each other.

China is an active member of the BRICS countries (Brazil, Russia, India, China and South Africa). Apart from their status as emerging countries, the BRICS have very little in common: China and Russia are authoritarian countries while Brazil and India are pluralistic democracies; China is a very centralized country unlike Brazil and India which are federal States; Brazil and India are market economies while China and Russia are State capitalist countries, and so on. Likewise, Russia and Brazil are oil and gas producers while the other State members are heavy importers. However, upon China's initiative, a joint development bank (New Development Bank) was launched in 2015 with a $100 billion paid in capital out of which $41 billion was provided by China.

Chinese Foreign Direct Investments (FDIs)

As Chinese companies are going up the value scale and are increasingly incorporated into the worldwide value chain, access to modern technology and distribution networks is crucial. A developing country has two options: either to develop technology of its own or acquire foreign technology. China is doing both. China built up scientific background and advanced technology in some areas but the key issue is to move from scientific knowledge to technical applications. Thanks to the huge foreign exchange reserve and the collapse of the Western stock markets, Chinese companies have been shopping around to acquire under-valued Western innovative companies, outbidding Western rivals. Chinese acquisitions are in the quest for industrial sub-contracting companies in critical areas such as car manufacturing, aircraft industries, aerospace and pharmaceutical industries. Now Chinese investors are widening their range of prospects to new sectors such as food, tourism, shipping, infrastructures, mining, shipyards and even movies. Wanda Group (real estate, media) owned by Wang Jian lin, acquired the American distribution network MAC Theater, and the Legendary Studios, a production company (that produced *Jurassic Park*) for $3.5 billion. On top of foreign direct investments, the Chinese are diversifying their portfolios with the acquisition of financial assets. However, the distinction between industrial assets and financial assets is increasingly blurred.

ChemChina, a chemical company (fertilizer, seeds), has been very active in the acquisition market and came to light in 2015 when the Chinese conglomerate attempted to acquire the Swiss agro-chemical firm, Syngenta, through a $42 billion bid, the largest foreign acquisition of a foreign company so far. ChemChina's parent company, China National Bluestar Corp., was created in 1984 by Ren Jian xin, an official from the Ministry of Chemistry, thanks to a Rmb 10,000 ($1500) government soft loan. Over the last few years, ChemChina took over Adisseo and Rhodia (France), Qenos (Australia), Elkem (Norway) and Adama (Israël). In 2015 ChemChina purchased the German machine tool company, Krauss Maffie, for $1 billion, and took a 12% stake in Mercuria, a Swiss commodity broker. On several occasions, Mr Ren stated that he has no connections whatsoever with the government, although the parent company, Bluestar, is one of the 107 State companies owned by the government's holding SASAC (State Assets Supervision & Administration Commission). In 2016, Midea, a manufacturer of electric appliances, made a $4.5 billion bid for the German robot maker, KUKA.

Thanks to a heavily centralized financial structure, China is in a position to back up direct foreign investments through a wide range of financial institutions. Every foreign investment must be screened and approved by the influential NDRC (National Development and Reform Commission) that reports straight to the State Council. Each financing package puts together a wide range of contributions—soft loans, long-term credit lines, export credit, project finance—provided by a wide range of financial institutions—State banks (ICBC, CCB, BOC, ABC and BOCOM), investment banks (CITIC, CICC), development banks such as CDB (China Development Bank), export-import finance (CEXIM Bank), institutional investors such as CIC (China Investment Company), NSSF (National Social Security Fund), SAFE (State Agency of Foreign Assets) and the newly created development banks sponsored by China such as AIIB (Asia Infrastructure Investment Bank) and NDB (New Development Bank).

Following a very active policy of soft loans, China is increasingly facing protectionist measures from its major trading partners: the European Union and the USA. In January 2016, the US Committee of Foreign Investment turned down the acquisition of an 80.1% stake of Lumileds, an affiliate of the Philips Group, by a Chinese investment company, GO Scale Capital, for $3 billion.

The Yuan Monetary Area

Moving one step further, the Chinese government now aims to raise the yuan to the status of an international currency. The aim is twofold: in the short term to lead a regional monetary area, in the longer term to challenge US dollar dominance through a new Bretton Woods agreement that would rebuild the international monetary system along a multipolar system to include, say, the US dollar, euro, yuan and yen, and be based upon the IMF's SDR (Special Drawing Rights). Something similar to the former EMS (European Monetary System) where all the member currencies were floating within a "snake" (±x%) is envisaged. But the cross rate between the EMS's member currencies were computed after their respective foreign exchange rates against the US dollar.

A currency area requires the construction of an off-shore deposit base through the use of a billing currency, the availability of financial assets on off-shore markets and the opening of the domestic bond and stock markets. But the Chinese government is not prepared to relax its foreign exchange control over capital accounts. Is an international currency compatible with a non-convertible currency?

An Off-Shore Deposit Base

The first step was to build a yuan-denominated off-shore deposit base. In 2009 the Chinese government undertook a pilot programme of foreign trade yuan-denominated invoicing. Some 359 MDEs (Mainland Designated Companies), mostly government owned companies, located in 20 cities (including Hong Kong and Macau), were allowed to denominate their foreign trade bills (both exports and imports) in yuan. In the following years the new foreign exchange rules were extended to 67,000 MDEs from 20 provinces. In 2012, the MDE scheme was cancelled and yuan invoicing was extended to all Chinese companies. In 2015, 30% of the Chinese export-import payments were denominated in yuan, which was the most used currency in the South-East Asian countries, but made up only 1.86% of total international transactions, far behind the US dollar (41.73%) and the euro (30.93%),[6] and 1.1% of the central bank foreign exchange reserves.[7]

The invoicing currency depends of course on the respective bargaining powers of the trade partners. Under competition pressure, foreign exporters may be willing to invoice in yuan to catch Chinese orders. And vice versa, the Chinese exporter is subject to international competition while the Chinese importer is in a better position to demand an invoicing currency that wipes out the foreign exchange risk. Foreign exporters may be forced to shift to yuan invoicing to remain competitive. When the yuan is weakening against the US dollar, foreign exporters may be reluctant to invoice in yuan unless they are compelled by competition. But when the yuan is weakening against the US dollar, foreign importers of made in China products may be willing to invoice in yuan. In any case, while the yuan is weakening against the US dollar, it is still strengthening against all other currencies. In this context, the euro may be an alternative invoicing currency.[8]

As long as the dollar was weakening against the yuan, foreign exporters to China had the opportunity to hold off-shore yuan-denominated deposits in a strengthening currency. On the other side, foreign importing companies of made in China products were subject to possible foreign exchange risk without hedging instruments. Since the 2015 foreign exchange crisis, the yuan was weakening against the US dollar and the market was working the other way round. In addition, an increasing number of Chinese exporting companies, mostly State owned, are authorized to hold foreign exchange incomes in a foreign bank (Hong Kong) account.[9]

---

[6] SWIFT: Society for Worldwide Interbank Financial Telecommunication.

[7] BIS: Bank of International Settlements.

[8] Foreign invoicing is the most common way of laundering money: the Chinese exporter's invoice is lowered and part of the full price is paid into a Hong Kong bank account; vice versa the importer's invoice is increased and part of the price remains in a Hong Kong bank account.

[9] SWIFT: Society for Worldwide Interbank Financial Telecommunication.

Off-Shore Interbank Foreign Exchange and Deposit Market

Invoicing in yuan demands a well-organized and well-supplied off-shore interbank foreign exchange and money market where Chinese and foreign companies can hold their yuan-denominated deposits in bank accounts, buy and sell, borrow and lend to hedge their yuan position. The development of an off-shore yuan market requires the creation of an off-shore settlement hub. Hong Kong is the most suitable place as, according to the "one country, two economic systems" principle, the Hong Kong market is both in and out of China. Actually, the off-shore yuan money market is a closed circuit: Chinese State owned companies are holding off-shore yuan deposits with Chinese affiliated banks in Hong Kong building up a deposit base in yuan. Foreign holders of yuan deposits have the opportunity to either hold the income in yuan deposits in Hong Kong banks, in the meantime using these deposits for other purposes (settling the purchase of Chinese goods in yuan, financing direct investments in Mainland China or funding the acquisition of yuan-denominated assets) or sell to another foreign company that needs yuan currency. In the meantime, the yuan deposits may be placed on the interbank money market or invested in yuan securities.

From 2010 onwards, when Chinese exporting companies had been allowed to hold some of their foreign exchange income in off-shore yuan deposits with a foreign bank account in a foreign market, the volume of off-shore yuan bank deposits (Hong Kong) had been growing fast to Rmb 864 billion ($137 billion) in 2015. It is another closed circuit: Chinese State owned companies are holding yuan deposits with Chinese affiliated banks in Hong Kong that recycle (sell or lend) yuan deposits with other Chinese companies.

In order to supply yuan to the Hong Kong market, PBOC granted swap lines of credits against HK and US dollars to the Hong Kong central bank HKMA (Hong Kong Monetary Authority). In case of emergency, PBOC may lend yuan to HKMA in order to ensure a supply of yuan and stabilize the off-shore yuan market. Later on, PBOC puts together swap agreements for the central banks of the off-shore yuan markets, starting with neighbouring countries (Taiwan, Singapore) and with Western financial centres, starting with London as an alternative off-shore yuan money market located in another time zone.

However, the fast-growing off-shore yuan market makes China's foreign exchange and monetary policy more difficult. When the on-shore and the off-shore interest rates and foreign exchange rates are diverging (the two rates are obviously interacting), PBOC must intervene to fill the gap and bring the two exchange rates closer together. The gap between on-shore and off-shore yuan foreign exchange rates is a reliable sign of the yuan's strength or weakness (Fig. 10.1).

In January 2016, the overnight interest rates on the Hong Kong money market rocketed to 66.8%. Hong Kong banks could not buy or borrow yuan deposits any more. As a result, the yuan foreign exchange rate against the US dollar quoted on the on-shore and off-shore markets diverged: 6.6775 in Hong Kong against 6.5749 in Shanghai.[10] PBOC had to withdraw funds from the foreign exchange reserves to sell US

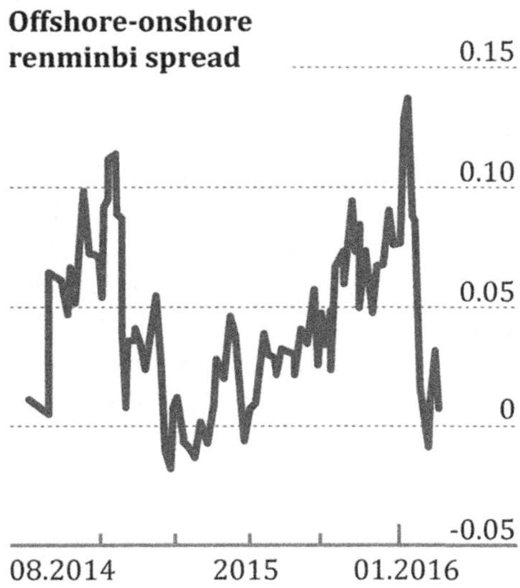

Fig. 10.1 Offshore-onshore Renminbi spread
Source: Thomson Reuters, HSBC

[10] As the yuan foreign exchange rate is "indirect", it moves in reverse order against the dollar: the lower the yuan foreign exchange rate against the US dollar, the higher the yuan quotation is.

dollars against yuan on the Hong Kong market (and the other way round on the Shanghai market) to fill the gap while the off-shore yuan's interest rate traded in Hong Kong was brought down to 8.3%. It is a very well-tuned combination of monetary and foreign exchange policies.

Off-Shore Financial Markets

Foreign trade partners will not be willing to accept yuan invoicing and the subsequent yuan deposits unless they have the opportunity to invest those yuan deposits in financially rewarding yuan-denominated assets. Accordingly, the off-shore yuan market had to develop the full range of financial assets: stocks, bonds, derivatives, and so on.

Off-shore bond issues have been growing fast over recent years: from $83 billion in 2014 to $130 billion in 2015, including yuan-denominated bonds (panda bonds). Most bond issuers are government owned agencies (e.g. the Ministry of Railway), State owned banks and companies. However, since 2010, the off-shore yuan corporate bond market has followed suit. Shortly after the 2008 Lehman Brothers bankruptcy, the Chinese government launched a strong recovery plan including huge government subsidies and bank lending. Subsequently, the massive cash injection led to prestigious infrastructures, wasted investment and over-capacities, not to mention the funds misdirected to the purchase of securities. The next year, as the recovery was well under way, the government backtracked. The Chinese companies which were big and profitable enough turned to the bond market, including the off-shore Hong Kong-based corporate bond market. Later, the range of market investments diversified such as short-term 1–3 year bank CDs (Certificate of Deposit) and long-term bond issues such as CDB (China Development Bank) 10–30 year bonds. Finally, bond markets moved to yuan-denominated panda bonds issued by Chinese borrowers on the off-shore bond market (Hong Kong or London).

On the other side, the opening up of the domestic yuan market to foreign investors occurred: foreign direct investments (FDIs) and financial investments through QFFI's licences and the Connect link, for example.

The 2015 Foreign Exchange Crisis

For years China was accused of deliberately under-valuing the yuan to stimulate Chinese exports at a time when China was the world's workshop. In the long run, the yuan had been weakening against the US dollar since 1993. Following the 25% devaluation of 1993, when the annual price increase was over 10%, the yuan kept strengthening against the US dollar, apart from a brief interlude from 2008 to 2011 in the aftermath of the global financial crisis. Since 2010 the yuan started strengthening again by 8%. All of a sudden, in the summer of 2015, China was accused of devaluing its currency against the US dollar. For the foreign media the reason was obvious: as the growth rate kept slowing down from over 10% in 2010 to 7.5% in 2015, China was weakening the Chinese currency with the aim of stimulating falling exports[11] and backing the growth rate. Media all over the world headlined that, "without notice", China had reversed its 20-year foreign exchange policy and was again devaluing the yuan.

In effect, the central bank, PBOC, intervened not to devalue the yuan, but on the contrary, to rein in the market devaluation. It is not the yuan that weakened significantly against the US dollar but the US dollar that kept strengthening. The yuan slightly weakened against the US dollar but strengthened against all other currencies which had been weakening much more against the US dollar. While the yuan lost 3% against the US dollar, the euro, the currency of China's largest trade partner, lost 10%: i.e. the yuan strengthened against the euro by 7%. Within a year, foreign exchange outflows reached $1 trillion. In 2015, the net outflow reached $676 billion. Foreign exchange reserves fell from a peak of $4 trillion to $3 trillion.

On Tuesday 13 August 2015, the yuan lost 3% against the US dollar on the foreign exchange market. As planned, PBOC intervened to bring the rate back to 1.9%. Chinese banks were allowed to trade the yuan within a ±2% fluctuation margin. Every day, based on a sample of rates provided by a group of banks, at 9:30 a.m. sharp, the PBOC picked up a

[11] In effect the overall Chinese trade balance, both exports and imports, fell in line with world trade, but the trade surplus, though halved, was still positive, with imports falling more quickly than exports.

"pivot" rate. In the perspective of a fully floating currency, the PBOC had been widening the fluctuation margin steadily: from 0.5% to 1% then 2% in March 2015. In spite of the wave of harsh media comments, the Chinese government remained silent. In an authoritarian country, there is nothing to explain. After a while, the central bank tried to backtrack. Exceptionally, the Governor of the central bank, Zhu Xiao chuan, made a statement to confirm that the foreign exchange policy was unchanged and there would be no further devaluation. A set of measures was announced to make the yuan more sensitive to market prices. From then on, the daily pivot rate would be the last rate quoted the day before. The yuan foreign exchange rate was no longer indexed to the US dollar but to a basket of currencies (the weighting of each currency was not disclosed). In turn, Premier Li Keqiang took a stand to reiterate that there would not be any further devaluation.

But it was too late. The wave of rumours spread around the world. Media were forecasting a wave of devaluations, a currency war, and the collapse of the currencies of raw material producing countries. In such a sensitive market, rumours are self-fulfilling. To make things worse, the media disclosed that Chinese property and real estate companies which had borrowed huge amounts in US dollars to take advantage of much lower interest rates were near-bankrupt as they were unable to meet dollar-denominated loans and bonds falling due.

On top of that the PBOC had to sell dollars on the Hong Kong market to keep the on-shore foreign exchange rate in line with the on-shore rate. As an attempt to fill the widening gap, the PBOC decided to put a tax on the non-resident off-shore deposits in Chinese banks. The PBOC had to withdraw huge amounts of dollars (up to $1 trillion according to Goldman Sachs) from foreign exchange reserves to back up the falling yuan.

To whoever paid attention to the foreign exchange market, there was nothing new and the yuan depreciation was unsurprising. Since the beginning of 2015, the yuan had been weakening on the forward market. China's balance of payment was already in deficit as its trade surplus was halved, as foreign direct investments decreased while Chinese investments abroad increased. The PBOC had to withdraw the foreign exchange reserves to back up the yuan's foreign exchange rate.

A yuan devaluation to back up an ailing economy was useless. A 3% devaluation is much too little to have an effect on the balance of trade. In the best case scenario, a 1% decrease in foreign exchange entails a 1% increase in exports within three months, i.e. 0.1% of the growth rate as exports accounts for 10% of GDP. Indeed, Chinese processing industries are importing most of the components of the exported goods. Given the very narrow added value, Chinese exporters have to transfer the prices of the input to the exported output.

In addition, the yuan devaluation would have been very untimely as the IMF was about to add the renminbi to the SDR currencies (US dollar, euro, yen, sterling) in November 2015. Finally, the yuan was included on purely political grounds on 1 October 2016, although the Chinese yuan did not fulfil the requirement of being fully available to non-residents. As a result, foreign central banks had to increase the weight of yuan-denominated assets within their foreign exchange assets in accordance with the SDR weighting (US dollar 41.73%, euro 30.93%, yuan 10.92%, yen 8.33%, sterling 8.09%). But the effect on the foreign exchange market was minimal, if not nil, as the central banks had already anticipated the expected move. In addition, the MSCI (Morgan Stanley Commodity Index) was considering including the yuan stocks within its index components. This was a critical measure for the Chinese financial markets, as a number of investment funds, such as pension funds, are forbidden to buy securities which are not listed within an index to make sure that the assets are always available and sufficiently liquid.

The yuan foreign exchange market and the Chinese stock exchange markets stabilized in the course of 2016 but did not recover. Now China is at a crossroads. To stop foreign exchange outflow, China either has to lift all foreign exchange controls over capital accounts, making the yuan a fully floating and convertible currency, or re-establish foreign exchange controls. The 2015 foreign exchange crisis mismanagement had adversely affected the Chinese government's credibility. An obvious lack of communication and a too late market intervention had cast doubt over further statements and interventions. Since then foreign investors are in a wait-and-see situation. To meet market price targets, the PBOC has had to resort to more ammunition to reach the same goals. This evidenced a certain lack of understanding of how the market works. The Chinese government does not seem to be ready to release its grip over the market in order to rule the economy in accordance with market prices. Sooner or later, the Chinese government has to make up its mind: either to keep control over market fluctuations, or let the market fluctuate in accordance with a bid and offer balance.

11

Conclusion

When Deng Xiao ping said that one must "*cross the river by feeling the stones*" he did not mean that one must stop in the middle of the ford. That is exactly where the Chinese government is currently. Once again, interest rate liberalization is on the way, but the rate schedule has neither been cancelled nor withdrawn, only amended. This is in accordance with the traditional Chinese though that prioritizes the path (*dao*) over the final goal, learning by doing rather than doing by learning. Since China accounts for 23% of world GDP and has contributed to half of the world's growth rate since 2008 (according to the World Bank), the Chinese economic transition is of primary importance to the rest of the world.

The global indebtedness of the Chinese economy is growing fast while its growth rate is declining steadily. The average return on investment is plummeting. As the growth rate is declining, the inefficiency of the financial system is increasing and the reform policy is becoming increasingly difficult to implement. As long as the growth rate stayed above 10% the Chinese economy could afford to live with a relatively inefficient financial system, but when the growth rate decreased and went under 7% (6.9% in 2015, 6.5% estimated for 2016), reform of the financial system has become much harder. If the Chinese growth rate is stabilizing at say 5%

D. De Rambures, F. Escobar Duenas, *China's Financial System*,
DOI 10.1007/978-3-319-40451-6_11

(which would be a remarkable achievement compared to developed countries, and would make China one of the fastest-growing of the emerging countries), the reform of the financial system may become increasingly difficult. Former Prime Minister Wen Jia bao stated on several occasions that China needed a minimum 8% growth rate to absorb the annual wave of countryside migrants and recently graduated students. In 2016, the estimated growth rate should be near 6.5%, far below the critical 8% growth rate.[1] In this context, the Chinese government prioritizes social and political stability over economic reform.

The Chinese financial system is threatened by fast-growing indebtedness: local governments, state-owned companies, property developers, increasing over-capacities (steel, cement, solar, energy intensive industries), sinking commodity prices and the growing indebtedness of related companies, salary increases at an annual rate over 10% since 2010, shrinking exports and the collapse of a great number of exporting companies that could not meet the competition of neighbouring countries with lower labour costs, etc. Mirroring the growing indebtedness of the whole economy, the banks' profit record is decreasing as well as profit margins (from an average 3% in 2008 down to 2.3% in 2015 and an estimated 2% in 2016), while the volume of problematic loans, whether they are qualified as such or not, is growing fast. The non-performing loans are growing faster than banks' assets. The value of annual write-offs doubled between 2013 and 2014. On top of the deteriorating quality of loan portfolios, the profitability of the banking industry is threatened by externalities: interest rate liberalization that squeezes profit margins, renminbi internationalization that increases competition, and rocketing internet banking and finance that is nibbling the market share of traditional bricks and mortar State banks. Fast growing indebtedness, which rose from 150% of GNP in 2007 to 250% in 2015, is a major problem for China's economy and may be the source of uncontrollable bubbles.

In order to relieve the burden of bad loans and improve banks' solvency, the government removed assets from the banks' balance sheets by securitizing problematic loans and spreading the risk burden from banking to capital markets. On the lower side of the credit range, banks

[1] Not to mention the widespread arguments about the reliability of the official Chinese data.

transferred loans to WMPs (Wealth Management Products), negotiable synthetic securities and trusts that buy back bank loans. On the upper range, companies that are large enough (mostly State owned companies and the largest privately owned groups) shifted from bank credit to capital markets. Local governments' bank loans are converted into longer-term bonds partially subscribed by banks, and partially placed on capital markets. However, saving instruments such as WMPs and trusts proved to be risky and the government had to regulate the new investment products. Due to regulation, the return from WMPs and trusts decreased. To produce the same level of return, banks' WMPs and trusts had to put together more risky loans into the loan packages sold. The government managed to cut off the link between the interbank money market and risky saving products such as banks' WMPs and trusts, as well as local governments' LGFVs (Local Government Finance Vehicles) that up until then used to be funded through bank lending. The government is actively supporting online banking and finance to lower borrowing costs and to allow small and medium-sized companies as well as rural firms and western provinces to have access to bank credit, and to increase the pressure for innovation on traditional State bank networks.

The final aim was to lighten banks' dependence on interest margins and to increase the share of fee income within bank profits. The tightening regulations increased compliance and risk management costs. The increased competition decreased banks' interest margins. The deposit insurance scheme set up on 1 April 2015 was another step in the same direction.

Along the same lines, the government tried to transfer government funded investments to private investors. However, in order to back up a steadily declining growth rate, the government turned to the most effective recovery weapons available in the short term, i.e. government and local government subsidies, policy bank soft loans and State bank lending, rather than resorting to private sources of financing as planned. In 2014, the share of private investment remained at a low level, 26% of total investment, the rest being provided by government subsidies and State bank lending.

Following the increasing internationalization of capital markets, government measures were mostly designed to repatriate the growing pool of Chinese savings that was building up off-shore (mostly in Hong Kong) back home, to bolster the domestic market. Most if not all of the Hong Kong-based banks, and most bond and stock issuers, are from Mainland China. It is a closed circuit that is recycling off-shore Chinese deposits and savings in favour of Mainland Chinese companies.

The combination of a long-term reform policy and short-term management proved to be inconsistent and in some instances contradictory. Following the declining growth rate, the government increased government subsidies and bank credit to infrastructure investment, which is inconsistent with the 12th and 13th Plan (the latter approved in March 2016 by the People's Congress) objectives to move from a public investment-led economy to a consumption-driven growth. Every time the government has to cope with an unexpected crisis, it turns to the usual short-term government controlled recovery tools and structural reforms are postponed.

Market volatility due to the government's erratic and untimely interventions keeps foreign investors away. Here lies the major weakness of the Chinese financial system. The Chinese government keeps a tight control not only on bank and financial institutions, but also on banking and financial markets: credit, bond and stock markets alike. Every time it has faced a market crisis, the government has backtracked to its good, old, stringent, top-down measures with the expectations that they are going to calm markets down. Not only does government interference not work, but it also derails market mechanisms. Market participants (public and private institutions alike) withdraw from the market, until they have a view of the government's goals. After repeated and worsening market crises, there is now growing pressure between diverging market mechanisms and government policy. China's State-Party is indeed willing to pursue the policy of reform and opening up launched 30 years ago, as long as the Party's dominance remains unchallenged. Sooner or later, due to these diverging trends, this pressure may become unbearable.

Bibliography

Barth, James R., John A. Tatom, and Yago Glenn. *China's Emerging Financial Markets, Challenges and Opportunities*. Springer, 2009.

Bayoumi, Tamin, and Frnziska Ohnsorge. *Do Inflows or Outflows Dominate? Global Implications of Capital Account Liberalization in China*. International Monetary Fund, 2013.

Bell, Stephen, and Feng Hui. *The Rise of the People's Bank of China: The Politics of Institutinal Change*. Harvard University Press, 2013.

CBRC. Annual Report, 2015.

China Financial Stability Report. 2015.

Chorafas, Dimitri N. *Capitalism Without Capital*. Palgrave Macmillan, 2009.

CIRC. Annual Report, 2015.

Cousin, Violaine. *Banking in China*. Palgrave Macmillan, 2007.

Craig, R. Sean, Changchun Hua, Philip Ng, and Raymond Yuen. *Development of the Renminbi Market in Hong Kong SAR: Assessing Onshore-Offshore Market Integration*. International Monetary Fund, 2013.

CSRC. Annual Report, 2015.

Cumming, Douglas, Alessandra Guariglia, Wen xuhan Hou, and Lee Edward. *Developing China's Capital Market: Experiences and Challenges*. Palgrave Macmillan, 2013.

Das, Udaibir S., Jonathan Fiechter, and Tao Sun. *China's Road to Greater Financial Stability, Some Policy Perspectives*. International Monetary Fund, 2013.

D. De Rambures, F. Escobar Duenas, *China's Financial System*,
DOI 10.1007/978-3-319-40451-6

Debelle, Guy, and Stanley Fischer. *How Independent Should a Central Bank Be?* Federal Reserve Bank of Boston, 1994.

Eichengreen, Barry, and Masahiro Kawai, eds. *Renminbi Internationalization, Achievements, Prospects, and Challenges*. Brooking Institution Press, 2015.

Friedman, Milton. Should There Be an Independent Monetary Authority. In *In Search of a Monetary Constitution*, ed. Lealand B. Yeager, Harvard University Press, 1962.

Fung, Hung-Gay, Gleen Ko, and Jot Yau. *Dim Sum Bonds, The Offshore Renminbi (RMB)—Denominated Bonds*. Wiley, 2014.

Gao, Jian. *Debt Capital Markets in China*. Wiley, 2008.

Hong, Sheng, and Zhao Nong. *China's State Owned Enterprises: Nature, Performance and Reform*. World Scientific, 2013.

Huang, Hui. *Robin, Securities and Capital Markets Law in China*. Oxford University Press, 2014.

International Bank for Reconstruction and Development. Development Research Center of the State Council of the People's Republic of China, China 2030, 2012.

Ji, Xiao Hui. *Shanghaî Finance*. Thomson, 2008.

KPMG. *Mainland China Securities Survey*, 2015.

Kumar, Anjali, Nicholas Lardy, William Albrecht, Terry Chuppe, Susan Selwyn, Paula Perttunen, and Tao Zhang. *China's Non-Bank Financial Institutions*. World Bank Discussion Paper No. 358, 1997.

Li, Yang, and Kuhn Robert Lawrence. *China's Banking and Financial Markets: The Internal Research Report of the Chinese Government*, Wiley, 2007.

Liao, Wai, and Sapawende J.-A. Tapsoba. *China's Monetary Policy and Interest Rate Liberalization: Lessons from International Experiences*. International Monetary Fund, 2014.

Lu, Yingqiu, and Tao Sun. *Local Government Financing Platforms in China: A Fortune or Misfortune?* International Monetary Fund, 2013.

Ma, Guonan, and Wang Yi. *China's High Saving Rate: Myth And Reality, Bank of International Settlement*. Working Paper No. 312, 2010.

Martin, Michael F. *China's Banking System: Issues for Congress*, 2012.

Maziad, Samar, and Joong Shik Kang. *RMB Internationalization: Onshore/Offshore Links*. International Monetary Fund, 2012.

Minkin, Robert. *The Off-shore Renminbi: The Rise of the Chinese Currency and Its Globla Future*, Wiley, 2013. Congressional Research Service, 2012.

Ocampo, José Antonio, and Joseph Stiglitz. *Capital Market Liberalization and Development*. Oxford University Press, 2008.

OEDE. Economic Survey, China, March, 2015.

People's Bank of China. Annual Report, 2015.

People's Bank of China. China Monetary Policy Report, 2015.

Ping, He Wei. *Banking Regulation in China: The Role of Public and Private Sectors*. Palgrave Macmillan, 2014.

Price Waterhouse Cooper. *Banking and Finance in China: The Outlook for 2015*.

Salih, Neftci, and Michelle Yuan Ménager-Xu. *China's Financial Markets*. Elsevier Academic Press, 2007.

Shich, Victor S. *Factions and Finance in China, Elite Conflicts and Inflation*. Cambridge UP, 2008.

Shu, Chang, Dong He, and Xiaoqiang Cheng. *One Currency, Two Markets: The Renminbi's Growing Influence in Asia-Pacific*. BIS Working Papers, 2014.

Singh, Anoop, Malhar Nabar, and Papa N'Diaye. *China's Economy in Transition, From External to Internal Rebalancing*. International Monetary Fund, 2013.

Taylor, John B. *The Effectiveness of Central Bank Independence Versus Policy Rules*. Central Bank Independence: Reality of Myth? American Economic Association Annual Meeting, 2013.

Wang, Jiazhuo G., Hongwe Xu, and Jun Ma, eds. *Financing the Underfinanced, Online Lending in China*. Springer, 2015.

Wu, Xiao qiu. *Reforming China's Capital Market: The Future Development Path*. Enrich Professional Publishing, 2015.

Yi, Gang. *Money, Banking, and Financial Markets in China*. Westview Press, 1994.

Yulu, Chen. *Chinese Currency and the Global Economy: The Rise of the Renminbi*. MacGraw Hill, 2014.

Zhang, Peter G. *The Chinese Yuan, Internationalization & Financial Products in China*. KPMG, 2011.

Zhang, Yuanyan Sophia, and Steven Barnett. *Fiscal Vulnerabilities and Risks from Local Government in China*. International Monetary Fund, 2014.

Zhong Guo Zheng Quan Jian Gu Guan Li Wei Yuan Hui Bian. *China's Futures Market Yearbook*. China Financial Publishing House, 2015.

Zhou, Zongfei. *Banking Laws in China*. Kluwer, 2007.

Zhu, Min, Cai Jinqing, and Martha Avery. *China's Emerging Financial Markets, Challenges and Global Impact*. Wiley, 2009.

Index[1]

[1] Note: Page number followed by "n" denote Notes

D. De Rambures, F. Escobar Duenas, *China's Financial System*,
DOI 10.1007/978-3-319-40451-6

The manufacturer's authorised representative in the EU is Springer Nature Customer Service Centre GmbH, Europaplatz 3, 69115 Heidelberg, Germany. If you have any concerns regarding our products, please contact ProductSafety@springernature.com

Printed and bound by CPI Group (UK) Ltd, Croydon, CR0 4YY
30/09/2026
02225565-0006